An Ethics of Sanity

Sid Prise

chipmunkapublishing
the mental health publisher

All rights reserved, no part of this publication may be reproduced by any means, electronic, mechanical photocopying, documentary, film or in any other format without prior written permission of the publisher.

> Published by
> Chipmunkapublishing
> PO Box 6872
> Brentwood
> Essex CM13 1ZT
> United Kingdom

http://www.chipmunkapublishing.com

Copyright © Sid Prise 2010

Edited by Aleksandra Lech

Chipmunkapublishing gratefully acknowledge the support of Arts Council England.

An Ethics of Sanity

Sid Prise is a writer and activist born in 1972 in Chicago. Sid was diagnosed with Undifferentiated Schizophrenia in 1997, following a prolonged mental and emotional crisis culminating in hearing voices, which he deals with to this day. He has been writing seriously since 1994, and published his first novel, True Faith, in 2003.

He resides with his partner, Kathy, and their friends in a collective house in Chicago.

Sid Prise

An Ethics of Sanity

Some Opening Thoughts

The term "civilisation" has been thrown around a lot lately, and like all words, all abstractions, it means as much connotatively as it does denotatively. People often use the term because it *feels* right to them, support or opposition to civilisation based as much on sentiment as on logic. Many people are proud of their civilisation, linking their identities to its identity as others may link themselves to their ancestral religion or their family name. Many others, without fully realising it, contribute to the functioning of their civilisation by their work, by what they do in their leisure time, even (some might argue) their continuing to speak their particular language. And there are those who, increasingly, oppose their civilisation - or the very idea of "civilisation" itself - through what they say and do. Most all of this latter group would consider themselves to be "radical" in some way, in that their outlook is geared to changing fundamentally what they see and experience in their society; and yet, many other radical people see the term "civilisation" as connoting something positive and good, something worth keeping - even if its present state is one they seek to change.

My intention with *my* use of the term is not to claim adherence to any particular "anti-civilisation," "primitivist," or "anti-Western" perspective; neither do I wish to distance myself from those who hold such views. To me, a radical perspective is the only one a person who looks seriously and honestly at the state of the world can come to, if there is an ounce of humanity in his heart or a gram of sense in her head. To radically change something is to change something at its root (from the Latin term "radix," which means "root"); and until we as a species seek to change the roots of the problems of our way of life, we shall be caught arguing over which "symptom" to deal with, versus some other—as if any leaf, or even a branch of the tree can be cared for, whilst the roots of the tree are dying! Radicalism, broadly defined, is the approach which seeks to answer not just how, but *why* our way of life is what it is – and attempts – as hard as it can be to do so - to answer that deeper question. My greatest hope with the following essay is to avoid the factionalism which has over the last forty years been so divisive among people of radical temperament, and if possible to bridge the existing factions into a more embracing community. It is not the time for splitting ourselves into rival camps over the use of this or any abstraction. If radicalism has the least chance of becoming an effective force for changing the world, to save our species and the planet from extinction, it will never do so by splitting itself further than it already is.

Civilisation, to me, denotes and connotes primarily class society, the kind of hierarchical, divided society we all experience today no matter where in the world we live. The root of the word civilisation is the same as the root of the word "city." This is appropriate, for many have located the origins of the hierarchy we experience today in the formation of the first cities. In the following pages, I've crystallized what I've learned and observed about this culture, both contemporary and over the centuries, into a critique of this whole way of life - not "city-life" per se, but the hierarchical divisions (and the divided self which is formed in them) that came to be the norm for most humans. For me, "capitalism" is the contemporary economic mode of world civilisation, and to critique it is very necessary for any genuine radicalism. But the origins of stratification, be it class, gender, race, or what-have-you, go back further than the half millennium of Western European capitalism. And I would argue that without the initial division - without the *habit of dividing* - that predated capitalism by thousands of years, the development of modern capitalism and its imperialist expansion all over the globe would never have been possible.

Capitalism is indeed to blame for many of our contemporary oppressions. But some of them, like the patriarchal (by which I mean the acceptance of the gender binary, the ranking of the male-bodied over the female-bodied, and all the hatred meted out to those who cannot or will not conform to it), the elitist (class) hierarchies, the privileging of the "intellectual" (denying those who are not "literate" or "educated" or "mentally fit" their full rights as people), and the oldest stratification of all - that of human over nonhuman life; all of these, our written history shows us, predate capitalism. Therefore, simply to confine our critique to capitalism ignores the bigger question, the one underlying capitalist - and all other - hierarchical ways of life.

The question is simply stated: Why is any individual "better" than another?

The assumption, rarely thought about critically, underlying this question, is that the ranking of people is somehow necessary. While the urge to rank people may be very ancient in our species, it came to have its current political gravity only when such social inventions as the state, its laws, and other formalisations of this bad habit came to be accepted as normative. Much of philosophy and religion, specifically in their ethical considerations, have hinged on this unquestioned assumption. The urge to define a human being as separate from a nonhuman being, and from there to define what a "man" is (as opposed to a "woman" or a "child"), to the habit of considering what a more "worthy" man is (as opposed to "lesser" men), all developed in tandem with the "advancement" of our species from the brutish, unrefined, "animal" existence supposedly predating civilisation to our current romance with the cultivation of artifice. The contempt for the animal is the basis for all subsequent hierarchy, the very genesis of the urge to ranking entities in terms of abstract worth. What is animal, what is natural, is not seen as simply undesirable; it is actually seen as *the number one enemy* of our advancement. And civilisation can be seen as the ultimate contraption we've invented to distance ourselves from the natural.

Many people have helped me write this essay, both personally known to me and people whose acquaintance I've made only through their writing. Of the latter group, a few merit mentioning. Although a person acquainted with his writing will easily see the parallels, I actually came to many of my initial conclusions about civilisation before I read John Zerzan. I feel indebted to him for confirming and expanding what I was trying to say, letting me know that I wasn't the only person in the world who thought things like writing and architecture had contributed to the distancing and schism present in civilised psychology. Another writer I am indebted to is David R. Roediger, who wrote a book called *Working Toward Whiteness: How America's Immigrants Became White.* The insights in that book combined with the insights I'd discovered earlier in the writings of Howard Zinn about the colonial American experience, to help me take apart the "white" mindset, exposing it as an engineered rather than an essential identity. I am indebted also to many feminist, queer, and race theorists whose names I can no longer recall, whom I met and engaged with over the course of my Women's Studies and African American History courses in college, my countless chats with comrades and friends over the years, and the many occasions of pillow talk I've enjoyed with lovers of various genders and sexualities. This is not to mention my debt to good old Karl Marx, and the many historians and theorists who have worked off his ideas; this debt to Marx I've paid back by rejecting the caricature called "Marxism" for the most part, which I feel is the only conclusion one can come to if one takes his method at all seriously.

The above acknowledgments do not compel me to be a "partisan" of any of these writers, to agree with any of them altogether. They are simply people, as I am simply a person. Like any people I meet and exchange ideas with, I strive to understand them, learn from them, engage with them. But in that process, I reserve my right to disagree. The one thing I've learned - and it is indicative of the privilege of intellectualism, which I strive to reject - is the tendency of a writer to think he or she has found "the answer" about something. Many of the above fall prey to this unexamined privilege-claiming, and this is where I find most of my disagreements with them lying.

John Zerzan is controversial among radicals, not only for the originality of his challenging insights, but also for his tendency to be doctrinaire about them. Like Marx before him, he has with his very consistent system of logic isolated an underlying problem with society, a problem to which he feels all the other problems can be traced. With Marx, it was the class composition of the hierarchy that was the key to understanding society, not the idea of hierarchy itself. With Zerzan, it is the division of labour, and the resulting advancement and dependence on technology, which is the primary problem. I feel these are simplistic reductions (as nearly all analyses tend to be). For me, the problem lies not simply in these aspects of living external to our humanity, but the ethics by which we've internalised them that is key. Zerzan's critique is an essential part of any sanity in regard to the world - however it is found (I came to my own insights independently of his, for the most part). Marx's insights are likewise essential. Class forces, or over-dependence on technology, or any of the other aspects of civilised reality which many talented and insightful people have analysed, all have a place in considering one's own critique. But on their own, they are not enough to heal from the six to ten thousand years of deluded thinking which our culture has encouraged in us. To heal, we must not think the "quick-fix" of altering some external will save us. To heal, we must *heal*; and this requires each of us to fight a private battle within to find out why we think and feel the way we do, a battle nobody else can fight for us. This is the essence of my ideal of anarchy, the essence of living as a truly actualised being.

My actualisation has been a process of engaging the above thinkers, the many friends and comrades and lovers who have engaged me also, and the engagement of the blinding lights and the utter darknesses that live within my soul. Madness, as some states of my consciousness and unconsciousness have been termed by some, provides me with a unique "picture" of how this society works, archetypes of this hierarchical culture, lesser gods and demons of my personal myth – the way I live my life day to day, night by night. This struggle informs and has been informed by the explorations of the following pages. But without some fine mentors personally known to me, I should never have been able to survive this long in the hells and heavens of this world. I should like to thank several teachers here, including Dr. Barbara Ransby, who early in my life gave me access to the heroes and heroines of the Black Freedom struggle, both famous and all but unknown, who inspired me through the bleakest moments of my madness, as well as affirming a revolutionary feminism which lets me accept myself for all that I am. I thank also Dr. William A. Pelz, whose comradeship has extended beyond specific schools of thought to embrace my radicalism as a cousin to his own, and gave me the history to ground my ideals in the lives of working men and women and poor people, my working class family origins not condemned by his academic mentoring, but affirmed and celebrated. Dr. James Block, who was dean of the Honors Program at DePaul University when I attended in 1990 through 1994, I would like to thank for giving me the vision that life is more than measurable success in financial, social, or even academic realms, but has to do with finding one's own vision, and endeavoring toward it, fearing not whatever truths might lie at its fruition. The stories we tell, he taught me, is the way most all of us find truth, and was the way out of the postmodern dilemma of endless relativism; and as a storyteller, I found my purpose in life, my first novel based on a final project I worked on years before in Jim's Philosophical Inquiry class. There were many other teachers I could thank here, but two more were folk who were not professors at my university, but visited for but a semester before going on with their own artistic and activist lives – bless them in whatever they do! These are the poet Lynda Hull, who taught me more than any single human being how to write, if ever a thing can be taught; and Dr. Lloyd Vogelman of the Centre For the Study of Violence and Reconciliation, who as a young man fought with his life against the Apartheid government of South Africa, and imparted the fruits of that ongoing struggle to me and my friends whilst he visited DePaul in the early 1990s – his greatest gift to me surely being a colossal expansion of my political world view and my ability to form them. Aside from these great teachers I met through my academic life, I should thank my first teachers, my mother and father, my sister, and all the elders and cousins and children of my family, as well as the many family friends whom I still proudly call by family terms of respect. Without their inspiration, none of the latter lessons should ever have been learned.

      I do not pretend to know the future. I do not pretend even to know the present in its entirety. All I can claim is my knowledge of my own delusions, and the methods I've discovered over my years to find a way of overcoming them. My delusions stem directly from my frustrations with this civilisation, and have taken the shadow-shape of the civilisation. Paramount in the architecture of these delusions is my place in the world, both in its shadow and its substance; and a primary task that lay before me and continues to urge me on in working through my delusions is the reckoning of privilege and power in my identity, and the identities of the hallucinatory voices which torture me. Though these delusions exist within a shadow of the real world – my own deepest mind's reflection and reaction to reality - privilege in our society is a reality of flesh and bone, bullets and blood. It exists simultaneously within us and outside us. Rejecting it requires the courage to face our failings, and a level of self-love and self-acceptance that gives us the strength and the courage to work through them. Without this work, no change outside will make much of a difference for human liberation. Trusting one another to do this work, and extending to one another the friendship to encourage this work, is the beginning of liberation, the pattern of relating that can destroy our current civilised assumptions - and, hopefully, ultimately replace them. To postulate a particular vision of "the future" has always meant distancing ourselves from others who see it differently. But one thing seems certain: however we define it or feel about it, the current place our society is now is not the one most of us would hope for. And a world where people and the natural world can live in greater harmony is not only desirable - it is essential for our survival as a planet. It is on this broad basis that I feel any worthwhile ethics must be reckoned.

An Ethics of Sanity

Chapter I: An Ethics of Sanity

I am a madman. For the longest time, years and years, this has been an impediment to me, a source of inadequacy and unhappiness. I was persuaded by doctors, family, friends, the TV, and much of the rest of my surroundings, to view my madness in purely negative terms, and to view myself as "suffering" from "chemical imbalances," which could be "corrected" with medications, therapy, and other treatments designed to arrest my symptoms and return me to normality. My recovery has been partial, my symptoms have waxed and waned in intensity; but throughout, until very recently, I viewed these torments as things simply to be avoided, hoping one fine day to be "cured" of them. Many madmen and madwomen can sympathize, I'm sure, with this self-appraisal; and indeed, there certainly is validity in wanting to be free of hallucinations, paranoia, mania and depression, all of which I've dealt with over my years. There is indeed much that is negative about my condition.

But very recently, after many attempts to think through and feel through and, most importantly, to write through these experiences of madness, I've come to quite another take on it all. Each person, mad or sane, is unique; their particular "snowflake" of personality and perspective is never quite repeated. It would be a shame to lose that snowflake, or miss the opportunity to view its beauty, to learn from its vision. I, like everyone else, have a vision, a message to share. And integral to my experience, something inseparable from the rest, is my madness. I have begun now to appreciate it for what it is.

The vision I've been blessed (and cursed) with is very dramatic, tortuous, and at times ecstatic. I've written more than one account of its dimensions, and the specifics of it are at times as baffling to me as they are to those who do not deal with them so intimately. My subconscious has imbibed much from my culture over my thirty-seven years, as has my more immediate conscious mind. This total picture, both from above and below, spawned the adversaries I face daily as my hallucinatory voices. They appear to me as four "characters," four personalities with names, voices, and attitudes which differ from one another; but they are united in their opposition to me, representing themselves as an elite, inner circle who run the world, and attempt to run my mind. It is not enough for me to condemn them, nor even to fight them. I must, if I am to become a whole person, resolve to *understand* them. This means understanding, deeply, the ethics they represent, and discovering alternative ethics by which I can live in opposition to their tyranny. How I've lived with them, and have come to a measure of happiness in their shadow, parallels the fight each of us must make to maintain ourselves in the face of the oppressive society that they simply mirror.

    The central idea, the discovery hard-won in the course of struggling to heal myself, concerns the schizophrenic split between my mind and my body, the paranoia which pushes me into isolation, abstraction within my mind that distances me from the world of my senses and leads me to question the validity of my emotions. When I am isolated, I am prey to all manner of hellish thoughts, delusions, and become vulnerable to the voices' tyranny. When I succeed in breaking out of this isolation, and become involved in community, I find this hell less intense, to the point where I am almost completely free. This schizophrenic condition is not, I feel, peculiar to me, but is the very source of the madness which afflicts our civilisation. More and more, the institutions of our civilisation - from the mass media to the architecture of our urban and suburban living

An Ethics of Sanity

spaces to the paranoid policies of our governments (anti-crime, anti-terrorist, anti-immigrant, etc.) - are trying to instill a fear of our neighbours, a competition with our workmates, and a cynicism about humanity which poisons any dream of a better world. Isolation is the source of paranoia, both personally and socially, and it is also its result. The vicious dialectic of isolation and paranoia feeds the clinging to privilege, the forfeiting of freedom for safety, and the perpetuation of a society based on fear and distrust. The only way out of isolation - within our homes, within our "niches," within ourselves - is to reach out beyond the apparent safety of our isolated existences to a larger community.

This dynamic is at the heart of my ethics. I escape the tyranny of myself by blending myself with my loved ones, and the People, whom I love even without knowing them personally. My voices try in many, many ways to convince me of the futility of this endeavor. They tell me that other people will never understand me, never love me, and that, further, my attempts to love the People are doomed to failure, citing an essentially cynical view of humanity, positing the fear of the People's betrayal, their backwardness, their prejudice. Yet, I have come to cherish my faith in people, in my friends, in the communities of resistance I live within, and in the politics which are based in them. And in so doing, I not only defy the voices' bourgeois and hierarchical exhortations; I prove, by my very act of defiance of their hate (by affirming *a revolutionary love*), that all people caught up in the system the voices represent so uncannily well can escape its snares by affirming the same revolutionary values.

These ethics I've termed an "ethics of sanity," for they have been the ethics of my sanity. While I'm proud to declare myself mad, and am indebted to my madness for the insights it has granted me (and the very immediate, almost sensual perspective on the evils of the society that drove me mad), I use the term "sanity" to describe my goal for two interrelated reasons. The first is that "sanity" in my personal life equates not to some "sanity" as defined as "normality," a nullification or disavowal of all the positive aspects of my madness, much less a conformity to some arbitrary standard of behaviour or perception decided on by "experts" who defend the larger society which drove me into madness. It is indicative not so much of "health" as *happiness.* Sanity for me is not the absence of symptoms, which neither therapy nor medication have ever fully alleviated, but a working out of their moral significance to me, reckoning my own morality in relation to them, and thus resolving the schizophrenic split in my personality into a more whole and healed subjectivity. Wholeness and healing are the only ways to be happy, to be complete, and this self-defined and self-discovered sanity relies upon and suggests an ethics by which I've learned to be free.

    The other reason for my use of the words "ethics of sanity" relates to civilisation as a whole, whose collective insanity caused my personal one. For many years before my breakdown, I had been wrestling with questions of changing the world, fears of my inability to contribute something positive to the fight, and confusion about how to view it all. While I drifted politically and spiritually, changing my mind more than once, even resigning from meaningful activism for a time, I still had a painful awareness of the evil in the world. My inability to look away from the evil or escape it, despite my uncertainties about what concretely could be done to address it, lead directly to my crisis thirteen years ago which culminated in my hallucinations. I plan in the following pages to describe the crisis, what led to it and what it taught me. In a fluid movement from the personal to the political and back again, I will draw a parallel between my personal madness and the madness of the society all around me, hoping in that allegory to draw a common conclusion about the dynamics of both. The ethics by which I have navigated my sanity are not a means by which to live in the world as it is, but a means to live in opposition to it. These ethics are finally an ethics of Revolution.

Now, "Revolution" is an even more loaded word than "sanity." It is a word, and thus but an abstraction, and its true "meaning" varies according to who uses it, who invests their own meaning in it. For some it is an event, an upheaval, an uprising which is worked towards as a future goal. For others, it is a way of life in the present moment, involving choices of opposition daily lived to commonly perceived if differently articulated tyranny. For yet others, it is a word to be avoided, as it is a fiction, a distraction, an abstraction so thoroughly co-opted by the system that it no longer has any value. And for still others, it is all these things, or none of them.

An ethics of sanity which diagnoses the world's madness must leave the specifics of treatment to the individual activist, to the widely varying communities of resistance, to implement. Unlike many who profess radical change, I am less interested in positing one or another program for action as I am in broadly and generally sketching the values by which a person or a community can act upon universal concerns, transcending the specific, logical political paradigms that currently divide radicals from one another, creating not some theoretical unity among them (this is neither possible, nor even desirable), but rather a brotherhood and sisterhood in matters of the heart. My hope is that this approach will bridge the divides more effectively than any vanguardist attempt at theoretical, "headspace" unity, by emphasizing the commonality in the heart of most every radical activist, the sentiment which only afterwards seeks the rationales of different theories and tactics.

I've been trying for years to put these insights down on paper, to come up with an ethics of revolution. But every time I've tried, I've failed, and I now know why. I was trying to "theorise" these ethics, and in so doing, I was creating artificial distance between what I thought and what I felt. This is the prime insight I've come to in the course of dealing with my madness, and it is the crucial idea that must unify any system of ethics I propose. For this *distance*, I feel, is the primary problem of our society, the very "disease" which infects our culture; this is the root of isolation and paranoia, its cause and its effect. The mad deal with it more immediately, perhaps. But the "sane" are caught up in it to no less a degree. Being a "functioning member" of this society is as insane a path as the many, more solitary paths towards what is commonly understood as madness. What a person must do to function in such a society, and what this functioning actually accomplishes on a day-to-day basis, leads to horrors so great as to be almost surreal. The standard of living enjoyed by many in the First World, the decadent overuse of water, foodstuffs, electricity, and gasoline, are precipitating a global crisis, draining rivers, ruining oceans, poisoning the air, and taking resources from the mouths of billions of men, women, and children outside the First World. The vast majority of humanity are either left to die of starvation and disease as the south of the planet is raped and pillaged for its resources, or forced to slave in dismal factories or on vast plantations, building and growing products for northern, First World consumption. And the effect of civilisation on nonhuman life is equally horrendous. The deforestation and desertification of the world drives countless species into extinction and threatens the global air supply for all; and the monstrous meat and dairy industries subject animals to unspeakable conditions throughout their short lives to

An Ethics of Sanity

provide a meat-heavy diet for those who can afford it, who are encouraged to keep it despite its basic unhealthiness and cruelty. In order to perpetuate this lifestyle, we have been involved in wars of increasing violence, have visited the darkest moments of genocide, slavery, the wholesale destruction of ecosystems, and the ferocious repression of any and all who stood to oppose these things. Now, clinging like a madman to a fixed and desperate delusion, we stand on the precipice of exterminating not only ourselves, but all life on the planet, and the prospects of saving ourselves from such a fate look bleaker and bleaker by the day. My voices glory in these horrors; so do yours.

How has this situation come to be? What has enabled us to commit these atrocities, and continue committing them? And what allows us to live oblivious to the madness, the utter absurdity which now threatens everything the last four billion years of evolution have given us? In such a world, is it so strange to think a madman's inner struggle could not parallel the wider world's madness? I offer myself, as just one average person who went mad dealing with the madness all around me, to suggest my path to recovery could be useful as an allegory for the world's recovery. And it is thus that I offer these thoughts on an ethics by which to live in this world.

Chapter II: The Roots of Delusion

Healing can only be accomplished by making ourselves whole again. All the problems of our society can be traced to the split, the distance, at the heart of our civilisation's psychology, and its roots are very old. From the very first planting of a seed in the ground, we human beings began to split ourselves from nature, at least in the way we had previously related to it. Instead of living as an animal among animals, taking our sustenance from the earth as all other animals had since time immemorial, we began some ten thousand years ago the project of "controlling" our destiny, altering the shape of the earth, and eventually our myths came to embrace the change. Instead of a relationship with the world of interconnection, we began to see ourselves as separate creatures, capable of "naming" the rest, and thus our gods told us that we were masters of the rest.

It wasn't long after the first agriculture and domestication of animals that the first cities began to form, and with them the formation and stratification of classes. This was a further split. Now, we were not simply separate from the animals and plants of the world; we began to be separate from each other. Also, with the settling down on the land, the concept of property came into our consciousness. Many anthropologists trace the historical subjugation of the female half of the race to the male to the invention and acceptance of this concept, because bloodlines became more important as property had to be passed from generation to generation. And metaphorically, our culture developed the schism between nature and ourselves into the schism between those more readily connected to nature (those who bleed with the cycles of the moon, those who are capable of generating life within themselves) and those more apart. Given the project of civilisation proceeding as it has, is it any wonder that the subjugation and contempt for the natural would reward those not "tainted" by nature over those who were? Women and men had been understood as separate categories even before civilisation, it is most probably true; but the hierarchical relationship had not existed to the same rarefied degree (at least not as evidenced by anthropological studies of the hunter-gatherer societies yet remaining, where "women's work" and "men's work" are indeed often understood as separate - but neither is seen as "superior" to the other).

Evidence also exists from yet existing primary cultures that the binary polarity of "male" and "female" gender itself, which civilised cultures now take for granted, might not have been the only choice available to people. Some traditional African cultures, for instance, had a "third category" of gender, allowing for what would be regarded in the West as "same-sex" marriages, particularly between males. Many North American Indian nations recognised and continue to celebrate gender identities other than the binary enforced by contemporary European cultures. Many nations have words for such "third" and "fourth" gendered folk, known in some communities as "two-spirited" people, specific terms from Native American cultures including "winkte," "nadle," "siange" - and many others. These folk may dress in a mixed-gendered or other-gendered way, and may or may not engage in sexualities which the dominant cultures would term "homosexual" or "bisexual." Rather than encountering persecution for their differences, traditional indigenous cultures such as the native folk of North America would accord these individuals a high respect, even a spiritual status of distinction within the tribe. It is a well-documented phenomenon in indigenous cultures throughout the world that shamans, who can be either male or female-bodied, will often assume another gender's clothing, mannerisms, and sexualities, in order to gain spiritual insight and power. These hints from contemporary and recent indigenous societies suggest that pre-civilised existence was not only one of greater gender equality, but of greater gender fluidity as well. This fluidity, as well as the equality, disappeared with civilisation's triumph over earlier ways of life. The social, external split between the genders (however many of them there originally were, from people to people, place to place) caused a split within the psychology of those defined by them, limiting the potential sexual subjectivity of human beings into the rigid and hierarchical binary which persists to this day.

The schism, the schizophrenic split at the root of civilisation's psychological makeup, begins with the separation of humans from the rest of the world, continues with the development of hierarchy of class and gender (as well as "gendered" sexuality), and then proceeds to the next stage: writing. This is the invention which initially, historians tell us, was merely cuneiform markings on clay tablets to record sales of grain. Trade, hoarding, eventually money – all were developments of further splits between people. But what writing became was the furthering of the abstraction of thinking, beyond simple spoken language, which had been with us for a long while. Instead of storytelling round the campfire, an intrinsically communal experience, the possibility now existed for the transformation of this experience into one of isolation. One reads alone. One most often does not know the author of the writing personally, and that author also writes alone. The isolating tendency of this kind of communication, in contrast to the older, more communal forms of communication, became possible at this point.

Of course, this is not all. With the invention of writing came the privileging not only of literacy (dividing people further into the literate and the illiterate - eventually between the "educated" and the "uneducated," with all the class inequality this division continues to perpetuate today), but of the very method of thinking which we might call "abstract." Literate societies went on to develop whole branches of "thinking" which split themselves off from the rest of living, and in the ethos already extant in civilisation, they became encoded into all manner of hierarchy. Recording trade led to recording (and formulating) laws; and then abstraction followed into mathematics, history, eventually philosophy and the sciences. Here now, the privileged members of civilisation, and to some extent all the members of civilised society, could justify further their separateness from animal life by glorifying abstract thinking. The very worth of the human person, so philosophers have told us since there were philosophers, lies in his (my use of the pronoun is deliberate) capacity to theorise, to abstract from reality, and to otherwise indulge his "higher" mind. This definition of man is still very much in vogue, of course. As long as civilisation continues, it will go unquestioned.

The social ramifications within the species are easy to realise. If man is the "thinking animal," then it follows that those who display greater abilities in this direction are "more" men than others. Thus the longstanding romance with the genius, the intellectual, the thinker. And, as a shadow image to this, we have the "lesser" men, those whom class forces have rendered into the role of manual, "menial" labour. Into this "lesser" category of person were rendered also women in general, foreigners ("barbarians," whose name derives from the "bar-bar" that the settled peoples of the Greek city-states thought the non-Greek tribalists spoke in lieu of proper speech) who did not know the privileged language and its writing, and by extension children, the mad, the mentally challenged, and others judged "unfit" to share in this exclusive fraternity of the knowledgeable. Athens, that quintessential archetype of "civilised" society, an ideal for many in our culture who are educated and intellectual, was a society where a vast population was enslaved and kept in misery so that a few thousand "citizens" could enjoy the good life of abstract thinking. And in later generations, as civilisation became even more degraded from the perspective of decency (i.e., as society "evolved" to new "heights"), whole continents were brought into conditions of misery on a scale previously unknown, and whole races were equated with the animal in order to facilitate their exploitation by early developing European capitalism. These people were raped, murdered, and mutilated on the scale of hundreds of millions over hundreds of years. The justification? They could not "think" to the same extent as the civilised, as evidenced by their lack of writing and technology and other traditions of abstraction, and therefore they were not as human. And of course, it was already a given long ages past that if something is not human, it is there only to be exploited and subjugated. Thus some of the worst crimes against humanity came as a direct result of this privileging of abstraction and literacy; and contemporary world civilisation would not be anywhere near as capable of producing wealth if it were not for the four hundred years of unpaid African labour at its base, not to mention the five hundred years of the extermination and displacement of the indigenous American peoples in order to provide land for cultivation and settlement.

We come then to racism as a natural result of civilisation's "evolution." Classism and sexism were earlier steps on the journey. All of them are the results of this fundamental distancing of mind and body, artifice and nature, the rational principle and the intuitive, emotional, sensual aspects of ourselves. The parallel between a personal madness and social madness is

An Ethics of Sanity

self-evident. The isolating tendencies, the delusions of grandeur, the anhedonia (the inability to feel and experience pleasure), the paranoia of the privileged against the rest - all these are signs of madness, the schizophrenic condition which I myself experience, and which my culture has been progressively deteriorating into for the past ten thousand years.

The romance with abstraction is the product of civilised thought. It is not "evolution" in the sense of a moral growth toward positive change. It is as easily characterized as a decline in moral value, for its genesis was in the context of an increasingly brutal society. One can say many things in criticism of hunter-gatherer societies' "savagery." But genocide, widespread systems of slavery, government repression, gross wealth inequality, and vast environmental destruction - these sins cannot be laid on our aboriginal ancestors' heads. They are civilised developments. Abstract thinking, and its further and further development away from the concrete, physical, sensual world, has been praised as one of the cardinal achievements of our culture. Yet, what is it, but a process of increasing dissociation? Deterioration into what psychologists call "magical thinking," patterns of thought which exist completely divorced from reality (something which I myself have been diagnosed with, and suffer much pain from)? Is it so strange a thought to connect the development and the privileging of such abstraction with the simultaneous occurrence of the brutalities we have come to accept as necessary to our project of civilisation? If slavery had not existed much prior to the building of the first cities, the first pyramids and ziggurats, is it so odd to note that the building of these structures required also the first "higher" mathematics? And from the first architecture (and slavery) to the industrial efficiency of the modern technologies of death (the World Wars, the Holocaust, nuclear proliferation, the widespread poisoning of entire ecosystems), our "higher" minds and our most degraded actions have kept in step with one another.

An Ethics of Sanity

Chapter III: The Delusion of Privilege

We have seen the result of civilisation's "rise," and have noted the connection between that which makes us more "human" in civilisation's definition of what that means - the capacity for abstraction - and the atrocities which grow more heinous with every "improvement" in civilised existence. We have seen the result of this peculiar privileging of abstract thinking for the many millions who were not considered capable of engaging in it. There is a temptation to throw away this abstraction, and all the things it has achieved, to glory in the "irrational" urge of the oppressed to riots and revolution—and it is not my intention to take anyone to task for giving in to this temptation. But just as I had not only to *resist* the forces of my mind, these abstractions which became my tormenting voices, but also to try to *understand* them, so I think that it is necessary to free us from the madness of this civilisation to examine the mindset which most directly benefits from and defends it. It is important not simply to empower the powerless, but also to analyse the most delusional of all - those who have privilege in the civilised structure of our world. The madness of privilege in our culture, the mindset enabling privilege to exist, must be diagnosed if we are all to be free.

In the course of battling my voices, I was confronted with the ways I was privileged by my culture, as well as the ways I was disadvantaged. It is not too much to say that my entire facticity was called into question, and it was done by characters who represented themselves to me as among the most privileged in my society. The voices represent themselves to me as members of "the ruling elite," "the inner circle," the same ruling clique that my schizophrenic father schooled me about from a young age, the ones who he believed had followed, tested, and judged him for longer than I've been alive. They confronted me, glorying in their privilege, daring me to resist. And they appealed to me to claim patriarchal, racial, or educational privilege as sources of strength and pride in my fight against them. (For they used *their* privileges against me.) But for one reason or another, I refused these sources of supposed strength, because I identified in my heart with those not privileged in these ways. Further, I maintained a faith that the privileges being afforded me would separate me from the communities I identified with and admired as more radical than my own. In so doing, I got first hand insight into the psychology of both the voices' identities of privilege, and my own. Parts of myself I had taken as a given all my life became abstracted from me, desensualized, becoming just one or another premise in an ever-spiraling and ever more convoluted argument. Yet I was made to feel a fool and a liar for not *feeling* my identities or my rejections and rebellions against them—and this added to my pain, for I could not even be assured of the validity and integrity of the pain.

I began to feel that I was a case-study in the abstractions and dissociations of modern Western man, and I began to see my situation as less a plight of parallels as a porous interrelation of microcosm and macrocosm. What is the result of thirteen long years of this dissociation in my personal psychology? What is the result of centuries and millennia of dissociative abstraction from the natural in the world around me? What psychology is developed by the constant symbolisation of reality, rather than the blending and bleeding together of perception until wholeness is achieved, harmony between mind and body, thought and feeling, the physical, "lower" self and the "higher" spirit?

Concrete, organic relations must be shunned if

one is to continue to abstract and objectify reality. Said another way, the sensual and natural must be suppressed, even despised, if one is to maintain oneself as a "thinking" being. A whole philosophy has been built on this foundation, extending through religious, political, and social dogmas, stated and restated throughout history. It has to do with disgust with the natural, and the obsession toward the "elevation" of the self into something other than natural. The schism between human beings and nature, leading to this disgust and distrust of nature and what is natural in ourselves, is furthered in the delusions of privilege, and these proceed to a deterioration and a derangement of perception which fuels the perpetuation of a society of madness.

The Delusion of Masculinity

Our system of privilege dates back to our initial isolation from the community of life. All privileges from that point on, beginning with the privileging of the human over the nonhuman, have had to do with varying degrees of isolation. "Man," almost the world over in civilised societies, is defined as being rational, in suppressing his emotions, in excelling in abstract or mechanical (artificial) aptitudes, of being physically strong (defined as isolation from pain and indifference to suffering and fatigue), of favoring ideas like honour and patriotism over personal relationships, and in general being willing to exert force over his enemies. "Woman," then, becomes the receptacle of all that is Other to man. She is natural, and in that needs to be dominated, "tamed." She is "irrational," prone to moods, capable of "hysteria," preferring relationships to abstract ideas, etc. This has been the narrative of civilisation for a long while, and versions of the stereotypes can be found in civilised cultures the world over.

Those who deviate from these predefined roles encounter persecution, not only because they frustrate the order, reminding one that the sex roles are not universal, thus threatening the crucial paradigm, but also because they are seen as frightening symbols of nature or nature warped. Queer men are seen as weak and unnatural precisely because they are *too natural*, too *womanly*, to be countenanced. And queer women are aberrations, upstarts who claim those positions which are thought to be the domain and property of (straight) men.

All the other gender possibilities are flatly ruled out, their expression met with disdain, their very existence denied. Homophobia, and the hatred and fear of all sexualities which defy the gender binary, connects

An Ethics of Sanity

with the oppression of women generally in the basic psychology of schizophrenic anhedonia and mind/body split that is at the heart of masculine privilege.

In order to continue to be privileged by the culture, the man is required to maintain a highly unnatural, strained and forced front of masculinity, a construct taught him early, encouraged with everything from blue baby clothes at birth (to use a Western example) to reprimands from adults and peers as he grows older when he cries. The construct is so entrancing and totalising that it seems "natural," and only with great insight and self-reliance is the boy able to escape it. And, even if he can find the psychological strength needed to transcend his role and become more whole and human, his society offers him a variety of privileges to entice him to forgo the exploration, to forfeit the liberation. Along with the enticements of privilege, the society offers early on in the boy's life definite penalties for choosing to reject them. The level of discourse available to the boy growing up with his fellow boys is not often one that is conducive to expressions of doubt about masculinity. Often this is the most feared kind of discourse, leading to ridicule and ostracism, even to violence, if it is risked. And most times, the company of girls is not available to him to the same degree, as a definite effort is made by adult society to separate the "sexes" into alien and even hostile camps. Even when boys and girls do interact, it is most often with a consciousness of difference, which only increases with the social pressures accompanying the onset of puberty. Isolation within himself, the inability to express doubt about the social role being foisted on him, becomes a crucial part of the psychology of the boy growing into manhood.

Meanwhile, the boy comes to know that if he swallows his doubts and "gets with the programme," he will be granted certain things which are attractive to a personality that has never been allowed true autonomy or a sense of self-worth. If the only way out of isolation is conformity, the choice to resist the sex-role the boy has been assigned is most often a lonely path, if not a dangerous one. In compensation for the suppression of his feelings, his isolation with his inexpressible doubts about himself, the masculine role offers him a sense of "rights" which are insidiously alluring. He comes to learn his privilege as his reward for having grown from boy to man, a process painful even in the luckiest, and this unhealed and unaddressed pain becomes a core reason why he clings to his privilege as a compensation.

The rights of the man are many, from a subtle but definite respect for his personal space, a greater freedom from sexual aggression against his person, a valuing of his opinions and an encouragement given him to express them, eventually better pay and greater job security in comparison to those not given his status, and finally the promise of sexual gratification at the expense of women. Pornography, prostitution, marriage, and in the ultimate degree, rape - all these are part of the package of privilege allowed him, and it is this that the masculine identity offers to cajole him into defending the system of oppression in which he lives.

But what is the cost? The masculine psychology is obliged in these appeasements offered by culture not to deviate from a rather narrow realm of expression. He cannot, for instance, look openly to other men for sex, much less for romantic relationships. He cannot, within certain limits, play the passive role with women (or men), even if that is his fantasy. He cannot himself be feminine, or gender-queer, or in any other way express his potential uniqueness if it does not fit the masculine mould. He is expected to "perform," sexually, occupationally, and in war. If he fails to perform in these realms, he is made to feel like "less of a man" - something which, without a firm autonomous identity of his own, will condemn him to a life without dignity. He may even be persuaded to end his life - if that life is not ended for him by other men. He must always conceive of sexuality as something he must "get," in contrast to the calmer notion that he can choose freely whether to seek fulfillment or not. A disgust with himself must be fostered, a basic feeling of incompleteness, a dissatisfaction which can only be assuaged by an elusive connection with women, which becomes for him an obsession.

The man is discouraged from seeking self-fulfillment, his exploration of his body enshrouded by shame and disgust. He cannot, for a moment, be allowed to think he has beauty in himself; rather, he must early on identify with the unstated but definite myth of masculine ugliness pervasive in his culture. The image of Woman is the one which is objectified to sell everything from cars to wars; images of men are rarely used this way, for the reason that in the code of the culture, his body is less valued. Woman is equated with sex; Man is defined as powerful if he can "get" the Woman, his most prized "possession." Rarely is he thought of as a "possession" himself, for he is in himself quite worthless. His masculinity must be "proven," to himself and to others, by acts of acquisition and power over women. Women, on the other hand, do not "prove" their femininity in the same way; rather, their identity is taken for granted, imposed upon them; and it is this femininity that exists as a commodity, precious, symbolic, with the masculine exhorted to be its sole purchaser and proprietor. He "needs"; she is not allowed the subjectivity to need, but rather becomes herself reduced to *a need - his* need.

If the man is "ugly" and essentially undesirable sexually, then the rest follows. He can't be content with himself; nobody "normal" or "healthy" would want to be with him by choice. Thus, he must force himself on others, trick or bribe the "services" of women, which are most always understood as mechanical "releases" involving just one part of his physical makeup, denying the rest. This is one reason he has such contempt for women, as well as for queer men: if they desire him, then they desire something ugly, and that makes them "dirty" and disgusting. An additional aspect of homophobia is the fear many straight men have that they will be raped by queer men. This follows the general psychology of masculinity quite neatly. If the man is ugly and undesirable, and the only way to assuage that condition is to go out and get a woman at any cost, then it follows that rape is the normal, natural condition of male sexuality. If this is true, then how else would a queer man, being a man, relate, but to rape?

Woman, in this context, is both worshiped and despised by the masculine mindset. She is seen as the possessor of Beauty, with a power over him that he resents. It is this power that his aggression seeks to diminish, his very lovemaking a will to punish her, to demean her and deny her the Beauty which his culture gives her and which he is never allowed. The act of love is thus one of "thrusting" and "pounding" the passive, as if that were the only way to view heterosexual relations. Yet, could not the act of sex be likened as easily to the passivity of the male and the power of the female? After all, it is she who envelops and thus confines him and limits his movement. And female-to-male oral sex, which most straight men *and* women see as an act involving female degradation, involves in reality the possibility of the most sensitive and vulnerable part of the male being bitten off at the merest whim of the female. (Of course, this is not the narrative encouraged by straight culture, so these potential interpretations of the act of sex are often not even considered, let alone emphasised.)

Lesbianism is seen by the straight male world as

inherently more beautiful than male homosexuality - if its manifestations are there for his enjoyment, to "entertain" him. The prevalence of lesbianism in straight male pornography is not translated into a tolerance for actual lesbianism in the world, of course. Rather, it is a "spice" that titillates men, giving them a little respite from the poverty of the extremely narrow range of possibilities allowed in the straight male experience. Lesbianism confirms the myth of Beauty which all women are allowed (and required) to partake in. But the "lesbians" in straight male pornography are always "beautiful" by the same straight male standards, the standard of beauty which straight women also are required to observe. The vastly individualised beauty spectrum of the Queer world, which enlarges what is considered attractive in women and other self-defined gender expressions, has little place in the straight male corporate pornography machine. That would be too dangerous to its project, which is not "pleasure" - even for straight males! - but rather, the inducement of conformity.

All civilised cultures have had very definite ideas of what is "beautiful" and what is not. However varied the specifics from culture to culture and from time period to time period, the code is always reductive, involving just a few set variables, allowing little to the individual imagination. If the woman cannot (or will not) fit herself into these reductive beauty standards, she is assailed by voices of hatred, both from within and without. This leads to all manner of self-mutilation in order to fit herself, like Cinderella's sisters, into a glass slipper that is too small. Like the "ugly" stepsisters, she must do everything, not short of cutting off her own toes, to fit herself into her prince's ideal shoe. In the West, eating disorders, "voluntary" starvation-diets, implants of cancerous silicon and collagen, and the injection of Botox poisons into the skin, all compliment the uncomfortable high-heels and time-consuming mask of makeup which, among many things, is mandated by the feminine sex-role. The well-known Imperial Chinese practice of binding women's feet, crippling them for life, and the epidemic of clitoridectomies in parts of the Islamic world, while both heinous by Western standards, are really not a matter of kind as much as degree; the main difference between Western misogyny and non-Western forms lies in the fact that Western women are not as often mutilated by others, but are instead convinced to mutilate themselves.

The psychologies of Freud and others have long suggested the infant's initial sexual urges proceed in all kinds of directions, from its mother and father to its own excrement. Considering this, as well as the almost unlimited conceptions and standards of sexuality found across cultures and across time, there can be no universal "natural" attraction to anyone or anything. Whatever attractions the infant growing into adulthood finds natural in itself must have a great deal to do with how it comes to be socialised. What was considered attractive in Imperial China was consciously reversed under Mao through a war of propaganda. The images of feminine beauty in the West as offered by art and literature have similarly reversed themselves in just the last several centuries, from pale and ample to tanned and spindly - with the European phenotype, of course, the normative cast. In a better world, we could truly say that "beauty is in the eye of the beholder"; but as a social reality, beauty standards are a pervasive and seemingly natural way to rank people, to create a "beautiful" elite while condemning most people into the cruellest conditions of inadequacy and inferiority. These standards, though probably existing to some extent in different tribal societies before the rise of civilisation, came to have their contemporary homogenising, normalising, and limiting effects on sexual expression with civilisation's conquest of vast areas into monolithic cultural units. Civilised sex, then, is the colonisation of the mind and heart with very specific images, and the elimination of local variety into a few hegemonic "types." The viciousness of the beauty standard leads to devaluing most women and men, to a corresponding "ranking" of people as desirable (setting a price-tag on the "prettier," and providing rejection and ostracism for those deemed "ugly" or "plain"). The anhedonia which is fostered – desire measured by how well one's partner "measures up" to the ideal, rather than the organic enjoyment of sexuality in the person of a unique and compatible lover - leads to the development of neurosis - the only kind of sexuality possible in the context of a society of unquestioned domination.

      The masculine has long been identified with the cultivation of abstraction, in thought, in perspective, and this can but carry over into abstraction from various parts of his own nature, his feelings, his vulnerability, his sense and longing for his own beauty. A prolonged state of this kind of abstraction (and it has been going on for millennia) can but lead to a state of isolation, which is a prime factor in the development of madness. This condition, this inhuman, horrible way of life called masculinity, is both a product and an essential prop to the system of oppression that takes so many forms, even seemingly unrelated to this modality. "Men" are not simply those human beings born into this world with XY chromosomes and external genitalia. They are indeed often these people, but these people socialized into a culture of greater oppression, the civilised experience, which requires this privileged segment to sustain itself. Wars need warriors, churches need priests, and workingmen need to be tied down in marriage and children, or else be freer souls, better capable of standing against the system. Thus, the need of the culture for a privileged caste finds expression in this artificially engineered social role. And while many forms of feminism have criticized the whole project of civilisation, and offered their radical critiques, the more bourgeois, pro-systemic feminisms have only alienated men from the struggle for humanity men and women both must fight because of the sex-roles, and these feminisms have succeeded not in altering the system of privilege, but merely in allowing some non-males to ascend to the lower levels of the privileged caste, and rule over others within the civilisation's hierarchy. But first, they must be made to think and act like men.

This is repeated for all categories of privilege.

An Ethics of Sanity

The Delusion of Whiteness

Whiteness, too, is a category of thoughts and attitudes more than a condition of the melanin content of one's skin. The condition of "whiteness" is one which connotes a condition of acceptance of the status quo. Indeed, there isn't much of "culture" in the white identity beyond this acceptance. Whiteness is by nature a departure from more local understandings of culture. The forgetting of local understandings, the particular Old Country village existence, clan and family identity, religious and class consciousness in Old Europe, is the first step in coming into a White Consciousness, and its political significance has much to do with the experiences of slavery and genocide involved in the conquest by Europeans of the Americas. Up until that time, no more than five hundred years ago, there was no "white" race at all, as there was no "black" or "red." There were, of course, always physical differences between people, and the Ethiopian visitor to medieval Europe or the Viking visitor to South America would of course attract attention from the locals as an oddity (though whether this oddity was seen with defensive aggression, or rather with curiosity or even attraction for the novelty, would probably have depended on the particular case). There have always been physical differences; but the organising of these differences into set categories depended not on their simple existence, but on the social needs of the culture where they were encountered. These categories did not have their now-familiar political significance until the social realities of conquest and slavery mandated their invention. The consciousness of "racial difference" only came with the widespread *real* difference of treatment of the various populations of the world in racial ways. Until the settlement of the Americas and the contemporaneous

African slave trade, the need to distinguish between "white," "black," and "red" simply did not exist. And while the original European explorers of Africa and the Americas remarked on the difference between themselves and the people they encountered, they did not always consider the difference negatively. In fact, many accounts of these first encounters are surprisingly praising of the non-Europeans, describing them as beautiful, friendly, nobly innocent and pure. Clearly the contrast between these first impressions and the subsequent conquest and genocide that ensued of the other "races" speaks more to the necessities of developing European capitalism than it does to any "natural" hatred for difference.

The process of settlement and conquest was an affair of several centuries, and during this process duress as well as persuasion, and often even outright force, were necessary to enjoin poor Europeans to leave their ancestral homelands and come to the "New World." The division of humanity, the inclusion of European peasants and pre-proletarian populations into the same "category" as the ruling elites, based on the accidental coincidence of skin-colour similarity, was only a gradually evolving phenomenon. The consciousness of the average, or even the elite European in the medieval period had very little to do with anything beyond a specific village, town, or fief. The very concept of a "nation" is only the invention of the last several centuries, and for central and eastern Europe, its development came even later than in the west. So, the idea that a medieval European from somewhere in the west of England would see herself as kindred with a European from an Italian city-state, or a denizen of the back country steppes of the Ukraine, or a tribal herder of Fenno-Scandinavia, is historically absurd. The consciousness which exists today of a common "white" identity is only a very recent, and in some cases (cf. the

An Ethics of Sanity

recent Serbian-Croatian conflict) a still evolving one.

Even well into the 1700s, indentured servitude provided much of the unpaid labour of the Americas, and in that system of exploitation, African slaves and European indentured servants were treated in much the same exploitive ways. "Whiteness" only came to have political meaning when the European settler elites found reason to "buy off" the freed servants with gifts of property on their emancipation, along with the first laws restricting and then prohibiting whites and blacks from intermarrying. This was a direct effort to avoid such threats to their colonial power structure as Bacon's Rebellion of 1676, when blacks and whites in several colonies banded together against their common colonial oppressors, and for a brief time drove the colonial government from the area, burning the capitol Jamestown to the ground. Fraternisation and intermarriage between poor whites and black slaves had been a fact of colonial life throughout the 1600s. In order to stop this generations-old affinity, "whiteness" in the sense we now know the term had to be invented, and through force and through cajoling, white servants were made to value their pale skins in a way their forebears had not. The categories of "black" and "red," as distinct from "white," came to have greater and greater social importance as colonial society solidified and expanded onto the "new" continents, when previously rebellious serfs, vagabonds, inmates of prisons, poorhouses, and mental asylums – all the "social scum" of Europe forced to go to the Americas - came to be enlisted to help their masters in the project of conquest. As the years passed, these categories gained social weight to the point where they now seem the "natural" consequence of melanin distribution in various peoples of the planet.

Even as modern whiteness found its genesis in the "new world," several more centuries would have to elapse before all those now included under its aegis were allowed membership. The Anglo-Saxon "race" which had pioneered North American conquest was slow in allowing later waves of immigrants coming from Europe to share in its privileged racial caste status. And during this extension of whiteness, the potential always existed for solidarity among the new immigrants with the older nonwhite populations. What became modern whiteness was the dissolution of this potential solidarity, replacing it with acquiescence to a power structure long based on racism.

The Irish experience in the United States in the nineteenth century is perhaps the first great example of this dynamic of de-radicalisation and co-optation inherent in accepting the white identity. Beginning with an ethnicity which was quite literally equated with the hated black identity, considered by some to be less human even than they, the Irish immigrants were in various ways persuaded to identify with their Anglo-Saxon class superiors, to pit themselves against the black workers with whom they competed for wage-slave jobs, and to acquire a racism as virulent as it was ridiculous. At the same time, the Irish immigrants came to form power blocs in the cities, slowly but surely ascending the rungs of political power till they had assimilated fully into acceptance of (and privilege-taking within) the hierarchy. They in turn came to side with the older Anglo-Saxon citizens in their opposition to still newer waves of immigrants in the twentieth century. Southern and Eastern European peoples were restricted from immigrating to the United States until well into the twentieth century, suffering discrimination from the Anglo-Saxon "natives," as well as from the now-white Irish; but gradually, these later immigrants, too, came to be accepted as "whites" by the civilisation which had only recently excluded them.

During the process of accepting and being

An Ethics of Sanity

accepted into whiteness, and as a necessary part of it, older radicalisms, cultural practices, and use of non-English languages had to be forgotten, suppressed within the immigrant communities and even in the locus of the immigrant family. With the loss of these particular identities came the loss of a sense of otherness, which had earlier found expression in these "not-quite-white" ethnics' solidarity with nonwhites. In the political and cultural press of these communities at the turn of the last century, we find articles in sympathy with blacks over discrimination and lynching, records of common cause with workers of Asian ethnicities during strikes, and a general opposition to the "racial purity" preached by the Anglo-Saxon establishment.

In order to accept "whiteness," and be accepted as "white," these "in-between" peoples had to lose their distinctiveness and drown themselves into a melting pot. When they came out a few decades later, they were no longer "dagoes," "hunkies," or "kikes"; they were Americans, and as Americans, they were included into normative American-ness—which has always defined itself in opposition to the other, "darker" races, whose categories came to exist to define what it is not. This dynamic continues today, with contemporary immigrant communities in the United States and elsewhere reckoning their own position towards the power-structure, leading some to wonder whether certain groups heretofore considered nonwhite (and persecuted as such) will become "white" in the future.

Crucial to the engineering of "whiteness" is the requirement to forget previous cultural heritage and then to align with the anti-black power structure as every other "white" ethnic has over the centuries. From my own life experience, I can cite this process going on in my own family. My grandparents were "Belgian," and spoke the languages of the "Old Country." But within a generation, those languages and that culture was suppressed, not passed down to my mother's generation as part of a very deliberate effort to "Americanise." The result is an identity in my generation which is completely devoid of any past heritage, the only thing left being the blank "whiteness" into which all ethnicities in my heritage have been dissolved.

The history of my family's race consciousness is typical, too. In the past, anti-black feelings were stronger than in the present, reflecting a "political correctness" which has driven outright expressions of racism from family conversation (though code-words about "class" and "bad" neighbourhoods are still sometimes heard). I recall as a child witnessing an exchange with my Polish-descended aunt taunting my grandfather about the proximity of Belgian to "black" by citing the Belgian Congo - a comment which he laughed away as a playful insult. My Belgian mother and my mostly Irish father lived not in an enclave of either of these ethnicities, but in a semi-suburban community of highly-mixed European ancestry, the town where I was raised.

Expressions of overt racism were not as central to how this community functioned, and it was possible to be unaware of its depth so long as non-Europeans did not appear. But the community was kept quite separate from the black people living in the next town, and the one time a friend of mine from that town visited me, we were attacked by five white "neighbours" (all our age) in the park. The politics of my family, like most all "white" families in the United States at the beginning of the twenty-first century, is one of superficial diversity - some are "conservative," while others are more "liberal" - but all are of a fundamental perspective of acceptance and acquiescence toward the status quo. My friends who also descend from European immigration all report similar political consciousness among their families, regardless of class, creed, or political tendency. Like all

An Ethics of Sanity

of them, regardless of class, creed, or tendency, my family reaps the benefits of racial privilege in ways they are not even aware of. And all are suspect of the radicalism of communities of colour, which they believe can never include them. The perceptions of the hot-button issues of current non-white immigration into the U.S., the recent demographic changes in the neighbourhood where I grew up, and the anxieties with the prospect of non-English and non-Christian modalities in "their" country, follow the same general tendency "whites" have always followed.

The near-extermination of Jews by the Nazi regime more than proves that "white" people are more than capable of killing other "white" people, without much twinge of conscience. And the slaughter of the Tutsi by the Hutu more recently, and the Tutsi slaughters of Hutu in the previous generation, proves that "black" is no necessary unifier of conception either. Whiteness, like blackness, is strictly a political and social category, and given different contexts can be as meaningful or meaningless as the context dictates. Yet, there is something rather more universal in these categories when we approach the problem globally.

Civilisation has grown in various places in the world, through the history of conquest and slavery that is the long echoing strain of civilised culture, from Mesopotamia to Egypt to Greece to Rome, where people who we would today consider "black" as well as "white" could be found in the ruling elites as well as in the slave quarter. But the current masters reside primarily in the north of the planet, and much of the political identity of these peoples have been collapsed into a "white" understanding. This is the understanding, the perspective, of privilege in regard to the structure of world civilisation today. And like all privilege, it is madness. Its madness can be identified along with other forms of madness, for it has the same signs and tendencies: isolation, the split between one part of human nature and another, paranoia, and a subtle but essential anhedonia.

The history of whiteness has as its running theme the separation of human beings cajoled into identifying with it from those defined outside it. Slavery, extermination, and conquest are old stories in the history of civilisation; they are older by far than the five centuries we've been speaking of "race." But the gradual equation of "whiteness" with mastery, and the other categories with subjugation, has come to encourage certain attitudes which fit neatly into a madness that bolsters the greater madness of the civilisation which spawned it.

It is unnecessary to go into the profound cruelties of the African slave trade; other authors have done much to illustrate it, and it would take many volumes - more volumes than there are trees to print them - to do the subject justice. The dehumanisation of vast populations of Africa is obvious; but consider also the dehumanisation of the "whites" who participated. To transport human beings across the sea, packing them tighter than sardines into the narrow holds of filthy ships, throwing perhaps fifty million of them overboard to drown in order to keep up artificial market prices; then to beat, rape, and torture millions more in order to break their spirits enough to facilitate the slave mentality; and then the four hundred years of living next to and among people treated so inhumanly - an experience common to almost all "whites" regardless of social class, gender, etc. - all requires a project of social engineering that can only be accomplished by fostering a profound schism between human feelings, empathies, and conscience from the rest of the human animal. Whites were (and are) required to ignore - or actively support - inhumanity in order to remain white. Other peoples do not have this requirement encoded into their social roles. Black people are not required to hate white people (though it often surprises me that more do not). But white people *are* required to hate nonwhites, either actively and obviously, or by the much more common and seductive method of ignoring and obscuring the ongoing genocidal practices of their culture.

All members of civilised society to some degree suffer from the madness of civilisation. Even slaves in Athens, or women there, probably felt a certain pride in being "Greek"—i.e. not a hunter-gatherer barbarian, not therefore an "animal." Few of any race in the northern hemisphere would conclude that civilisation is to blame for their conditions of misery. This is the "fixed delusion" we are dealing with here. But the attitude of those identifying with "whiteness" (regardless of the particular melanin-content of their skin) are those who shun any ancestral memory of resistance to this fixed delusion, in order to affirm their present identity.

Whiteness can be defined as the lack of colour. This is true in a very immediate metaphorical sense. Anything that "colours" the identity of the average citizen of civilisation, be it older, ethnic idiosyncrasies, any sense of political or religious antagonism to the dominant culture - in fact anything of "culture" at all! - must be rubbed out in order to preserve a blank identity, a clean slate. Thus the lament many American-born whites have that they do not know their immigrant ancestors, their culture and language, despite the oft-surviving claim on the names of these all-but-forgotten European ethnicities. Thus the further lament (very telling) that whites "can't dance," "can't sing," even "can't fuck" like those they identify as "closer to nature" than they in their impoverishment see themselves.

European culture has long had a romance with non-European cultures, even as it has conducted wars of genocide against these very cultures. This is "civilisation" in its "highest" form: the necrophilia of murderers for the very spirit they are murdering. The romance of "white" culture for "black" music, for "Eastern" wisdom, for "Native" lifestyles, etc., is nothing new. This love-hate continuum can seem very puzzling, for it implies at the heart of the white person an unconscious self-loathing and inadequacy which can only be assuaged by immersing himself in the very cultures which he is engaged, sometimes at the very same moment, in emasculating, ruining, and annihilating. But this is to be expected. Does not the rapist superficially "love" his victims, or at least lust after them? The crime of rape becomes something many cannot understand in terms of power, because it involves an act which has everything to do with deep connection. But rape is *not* making love; and though the two involve the same action, the difference must lie in the perspective of the persons involved.

The white identity is one of anhedonia, of discomfort with sensuality, of "purity" from the colouring effects of living in the world. The concept of the "missionary position," that cornerstone of the abbreviated and limited "straight" sexual identity, was named for the puritanical Christian missionaries who forced their native proselytes to fuck according to one limited method. The vast realm of sexual experience which more holistic cultures had retained was threatening to the white missionaries, who had long lost their ability to be sexually free and adventurous. It isn't a case of indigenous cultures being "more" sexual than is normal, but rather a case of most traditional cultures being healthier about it than the guilt-ridden mess that came to be the colonizers' understanding of sexuality. Faced with healthy, human sexuality in those they wished to conquer, the whites of course felt it necessary to export their own unhappiness, along with all the other "benefits" of their civilisation, to suppress in their native converts the basic connection to the physical that the whites had made their raison d'etre to suppress in themselves. Sexual openness, sexual exploration, and all manner of comfort with the natural processes of life - these are some of the prerequisites of health and sanity for all people. Whiteness in part is the dissociation of the mind from the healthy human relationship to the body, a sickness requiring not only the brutal suppression of others, but also the equally brutal suppression of oneself.

The role of the exploiter must always be one of extreme personal poverty. In order to assuage that poverty, the exploiter must find a victim, in order to suck out the life from her that he cannot find in himself. The gendered male, as we've spoken of before, must be convinced from an early age of his poverty, his ugliness, his inability to remain content in his own person. He must be convinced that superficial pleasures - getting his "rocks off" - are the only ones possible. This essential isolation from his own sensuality, from his emotions, from his potential for true human relationships - his very *beauty* as a creature - is the root of his madness. Just so, the "white" person must, in various ways, be similarly split from her humanity. She must be encouraged to identify herself with others, similarly robbed, only on the most superficial basis (her identity with the civilisation, and her opposition to those whom she construes as going against it - the "criminal," the "radical"). Finally, she must be encouraged to find fear, paranoia, condescension, ignorance - in short, *distance* - from those with whom, under different circumstances, she might identify.

The oppressor, then, is not strong, confident, powerful, or self-assured, as conventional wisdom would have it. Rather, he is constantly in a state of fear that he will lose the battle to maintain his privilege, and does everything, including engaging in some of the most horrific self-mutilation, in order to maintain it. The masculine-identified male must suppress his feelings, policing himself against the possibility of betraying them; white-identified people must suppress their ancestral memories, forget their culture, and give fealty to an inhuman tradition which denies anything natural and consents to genocide. And while the oppressor, the privileged, tries to enjoy the fruits of privilege, there is a creeping dread constantly being fought in his mind and heart that these privileges really aren't worth the effort. Further, that the enemy - the oppressed - is actually morally superior to himself in some way he cannot define with his pale "logic," yet senses all the same. Thus, the emulation of "foreign" things to assuage the perceived poverty of one's own culture, class, etc. Thus the cycle of self-hatred that only serves to dehumanise the individual further, and urge the continued clinging to the delusion. And thus the profound jealousy of the other which fuels the whole project of hatred essential to the continuation of our civilisation.

An Ethics of Sanity

The Delusion of Elitism

Elitism is civilisation's first and most fundamental delusion. Next only to the division between human and nonhuman, class hierarchy is the most basic of humankind's schizophrenic schisms with the world, both within and without. It remains a force which ruins all other attempts at liberation. Feminism without class consciousness is doomed to perpetuate male supremacy. Even if the women who ascend to positions of power are physically and socially different from males, still they oppress others in the same way that males do if they refuse to attack the structures of power into which they've ascended. Racial and national liberation struggles also come to nought if class structure and its socio-economic foundations are not deeply questioned. The politics of sexual liberation, as well as efforts against ageism or ableism or anti-mad prejudice or any other loci of oppression, cannot exist in authenticity without reckoning the role of economic, social, and political privilege by which they are perpetuated.

In order to oppress, one must distance oneself from what one oppresses. One must "name" the oppressed as the Biblical Adam named the creatures of the world, and that name must be a different one from the name one calls oneself. One must employ abstractions; one must see one's victim not as that being truly is, but rather as a symbol of something else. The greatest danger for the oppressor is getting to know the oppressed as an actual entity; for when one really learns to relate to another as a snowflake, up close, enough to see that snowflake's uniqueness, it becomes very difficult to continue to apply the abstraction. Thus, even with avowed racists, sometimes there are one or two people of the other group that are known on a personal level, and become "exceptions" to the "rule" of racial inferiority - exceptions, because they are no longer seen as members of the enemy caste, a category whose integrity even the reality of one or two exceptional members cannot invalidate. The greater the distance from another, be it spatial, psychic, or social, the easier it is to oppress. And distance is best achieved by collapsing the entities one is dealing with into broad categories, inhuman, logical things which allow the potential of human warmth to be written out of the equation.

People in the northern hemisphere live and work and consume the wealth of the south, and in many there is at least a dim awareness that the relationship they have with the south is one of exploitation. But how much easier is it to call the vast diversity of individual human souls living there "the Third World," collapsing them all into one easy phrase that can be dealt with (or, more often, ignored completely)? How much easier is it to deny the interconnection that the "First World" has with everyone else, and instead deal with the lies and half-truths supplied by First World media conglomerates and governments in order to think about "those other people," who might as well live on some other planet? How easy is it to forget that, even beyond simple humanity connecting the First and Third world's people, that economy, politics, cultural borrowing (and cultural theft) links the whole world together and has been doing so for hundreds if not thousands of years?

Elitism — be it that of the "intellectual," or the "citizen" of the favoured nation or region, or that of the ruling classes — must employ abstractions in order to maintain itself. It is the most naked form of privilege, because finally there is no substance to the delusion but the very claiming of privilege itself. But, like all delusions, there are complex and ritualised and seemingly logical justifications for it that have evolved

An Ethics of Sanity

over the millennia, ways by which those within the privileged caste and those outside it are persuaded to accept it as a sensible reality. There must always be a way to disguise the essential arbitrariness of the elite's distance from everyone else. And, like the fixed delusion clung to by the unreflective psychotic, the justifications of this delusion have been cultivated so thoroughly over its lifetime that it has evolved its own languages, its own paradigms, a closed system of erroneous logic within which it cannot be easily shaken. Part of how elitism has come to its current, obscenely ugly extreme in the world today has been the embracing of the abstract as its own tautological worth. The capacity for abstraction, in other words, has come full circle from a byproduct of the hierarchical civilised experience to the very reason for the hierarchy.

When European feudalism evolved out of the wreckage of the Roman civilisation, the initial rulers were nought but gangs of thugs who protected communities of peasant-farmers from other gangs of thugs, and for that protection insisted the farmers pay them tribute in terms of taxes and fealty. Over the millennium that followed, the descendants of these gangs of thugs came to cultivate a mystique of "aristocracy," hiding their essential brutish parasitism with claims of "softer," "purer," more "delicate" sensibilities than the "coarse" and "rude" (i.e. animal) existence supposedly lived by the peasants who fed them. This glorification of distance from the hard reality of toil and starvation found expression in etiquettes of table-manners and fashionable dress, the cultivation of the arts of the time, and eventually the invention of "proper" ways to speak and write—all geared for nothing other than the engineering of difference from the ignorant, "animalistic" masses.

With the triumph of the bourgeois, or capitalist, ruling classes over their aristocratic forbears, these same etiquettes and rituals continued to be embraced. But in addition to these signs of inclusion in the dominant class came a certain fetishising of "usefulness" to society. From Adam Smith to Ayn Rand, we see an almost worship developing of the activities of capitalism - till now it is "common sense" in the Western world to speak of the "efficiency" and the "progress" of capitalism — and the "intelligence" and even the "hard work" which the current elites supposedly exhibit by their exploitation of the world. This basic lie of usefulness, which the capitalist elites have long claimed, is an evolution toward the embrace of elitism for elitism's own sake — the embrace of the delusion more totally than past eras. And, instead of some "Divine Right" justifying the current hierarchy, the institutions of "science" are often invoked in the development of a materialist world view, without which (arguably) the technologies required for capitalist development would never have been possible.

Science, and the privilege extended to it, is the most rarefied of the religions of abstraction, one that in a technological society takes the place of all other, more mystical, sensual religions. It was the source of ethnocentrism for nineteenth century Europeans, even and especially those who wished to use it to solve the contradictions of European class oppression. The reactionary racists of Europe could claim Christianity and "saving poor black souls from Hellfire" for their brutal projects of colonialism; the "revolutionary" racists, like Marx, could claim a scientifically provable progression from "primitive" to "civilised" to justify the same genocidal colonialism. Proponents of Darwinian evolution battled (and battle still) the resisters of its "truth," supposedly in order to free society from superstitious bondage. Yet with this same "theory," the capitalist ruling classes of nineteenth and twentieth century Europe and America could demonstrate

An Ethics of Sanity

"scientifically" the social inferiority of the workers and the poor, and their own power as the natural law of "the survival of the fittest." Further, they could go with this thought into eugenics, to tests of intelligence and sanity and other artificial forms of "fitness," to the "science" of racism, leaving the way clear for the rising Party-bureaucracy of Nazism to wage genocide against Europeans in exactly the same way Europeans had been waging genocide against Americans, Africans, and Asians for hundreds of years.

Communism and Nazism, while defunct as political systems in most of the world today, can be seen as capitalism's inheritors, the bureaucratisation of the world an ongoing and indispensable part of the process of capitalism's "evolution." Bureaucratic collectivism is simply capitalism purged of its last vestiges of romanticism and idealism, its gods and its notions of "rights" and "democracy." Strip utilitarian power of anything but its raw utilitarianism, and you have "management" for management's sake - and all the "tools" pioneered during the development of capitalism, from Taylorist work discipline to the consolidation of the media into a monopoly of propaganda - straight through to purges and gulags and genocide - follow a predictable, logical course.

Communism came into being as an attempt to do away with class division in the world. But it could not create the conditions by which class divisions could be healed, precisely because it maintained the abstractions which fuel them. The privileging of intellectuals and intellectualism, originally an almost by-product of hierarchal society (the "good life" the rulers could engage in rather than work) was preserved by the Communists, and became the very justification for their rule. They and their theories were to define and direct the social transformation to a "classless society." Working people, peasants, and the poor could not abstract their reality with the same confidence as the intellectual "professional revolutionaries" in the Party. Thus they were thought incapable (Lenin actually stated this in plain language in one of his polemics, *State and Revolution*) of advancing their own struggle through to revolution; they needed the "help" of these professionals to lead them to it with the power of their analysis. This despite the long history of lower class uprisings without the benefit of any outsider's "theory" to direct them, going back at least as far as Spartacus' slave revolt against Rome. But the power of communist theory was entrancing to people long taught to obey their social "betters" as, among other things, "smarter" than they were. And for those in the upper echelons of the pre-revolutionary society, the theory flattered those who wished to be a part of revolution, to be a part of history - despite their lack of connection to any meaningful labour or resulting oppression.

When considering "revolutions" in the last hundred years, even bourgeois historians uninterested in bolstering Marxism mention Marxist theory, and use the terms inherited from Marxist discourse to frame their accounting of the events. The "Bolshevik Revolution" in Russia is called that despite the millions of ordinary non-Bolsheviks who actually made it happen. In histories of that event, like events before and after it, it is the "leaders" and their "theories" who are remembered, not the millions of people who may or may not have even been familiar with them. The people remain categorised, whether by Marxists or anti-Marxists, as faceless parts of an equation. And whether it is Communist agitators spurring on "the masses," or capitalist governments trying to weed out these agitators, the agency of the ordinary people is not considered. The blame, or the credit, are alike given to Communists, to agitators – to "professional revolutionaries" (to borrow Lenin's term). "The masses" remain objects to be used - whether championed *or* suppressed, the abstraction remains - in this battle between two rival, privileged elites.

My point in bringing up these differences in feudal, capitalist, and communist hierarchal societies is to trace the thread common to all of them, something which I feel is an essential prerequisite to all elitism, and its most egregious delusion. This is the human romance with the artificial, the "rising" from the supposedly brutal existence predating civilisation to the "grace" of what we now know as "*Man*kind." Abstraction might well be our species' particular distinguishing feature from other kinds of life (it certainly seems to be a great addiction for many of us). But whether in the formation of etiquettes, rituals, language, or "scientific" doctrines — abstraction always goes hand-in-hand with the deterioration of our ability to live well together, and to live on this planet sustainably as one species among the rest. And as civilisation has "evolved" from the superstitions of Church and Kings through the materialist efficiency of "progressive" capitalism to the unspeakable horrors of "scientifically" planned communist societies, the embrace of abstraction has alienated humans from one another and from the world in which we live in more and more ghastly ways.

My further point in tracing this thread of commonality in all elitisms is to condemn what I've experienced both outside and inside my head over the years. When the schizophrenic voices first appeared to me out of the ether, I had been drifting in an apolitical miasma for several years following a very bad experience with a communist group of which I'd been a part. I had been stuck in the conundrum of wanting to change the world still, despite the betrayal of my former comrades, but being unable to embrace anymore the politics by which I had thought to change it. Very soon, however, after being attacked by the voices (who represented themselves to me as the ruling elite, playing a secret "game" with my mind), I came back for a time to communism as my way of justifying my radicalism in the face of their vicious arguments. Very soon thereafter, the voices gave me a grudging respect as I was able to demolish their arguments with logic as well as sentiment, armed with the analyses I'd once studied of the capitalist system they defended. They appealed to me to take pride in being "working class" against them, and I had a chance to indulge in a "reverse-elitism" against them (which I confess I indulged in for quite a long time when I was younger and a communist). I'd seen some of my comrades do this very same thing when I was in college, making other comrades from wealthier ("petty-bourgeois") backgrounds have to apologise and justify themselves in ways that were simply cruel after a time. At the time, I rejected the temptation to revel in my righteous poverty, though I benefited from the respect I was given even before I opened my mouth about something, just for my "proletarian" background.

When my voices attacked, and I defended myself with my former politics, I had eventually to come to the realisation that "working class pride," while perhaps a necessary stage for many people to pass through on their way to a revolutionary identity in defiance of our civilisation, can be the basis of hierarchy and cruelty and madness, no less than any other. The victorious Communist elites in such countries as China during the so-called "Cultural Revolution" of the 1960s mobilised on the basis of this cruelty against many, many Chinese (both former rulers as well as millions of poor and working people), and set up a system with this hate that was no less cruel than the imperial system they were so zealously overthrowing. I found then that I could not conscientiously hate the voices for being rich, even if they encouraged that hatred and rewarded me

An Ethics of Sanity

with praise when I did it. In a way, their respect of my communist politics was quite like the respect that the capitalist rulers of the West gave to the communist rulers of the Eastern Bloc during the Cold War—a rivalry, with much hatred, but an honoring for the will to enslave the proletarian and peasant masses—the poor people whom the capitalists hate even more than a rival elite.

As hard as it was (and is) to reject this privilege among the many my voices have offered me, I've found my true ego (still very much in formation against their superego, the voices of society and tradition and morality they are nothing more than the "voice" of) could not settle into elitism—even that which seems so apparently justified. To grow out of my crisis, to achieve a measure of sanity, I had to go beyond communism, and this gave me insight into how wretched a philosophy it really is—even apart from the historic crimes of governments which have claimed allegiance to it. Elitism stripped of all else remains elitism, I discovered, if it retains *intellectual conceit*.

The privileging of intellectuals and their abstract thinking arose with class society, originally as the "good life" the upper class could engage in rather than work. With every class society, from the ancient city-states through the rise of world empires based on slavery through feudal degradation to modern capitalism, there has always been privileged knowledge, esoterica, the learning of which is the unimpeachable sign of inclusion within the ruling circle. Even if the "knowledge" coveted and kept by the ruling elites over the centuries from the "ignorant masses" concerned such inanities as how many angels could dance on the head of a pin, still there was this code, and the guarding of it became the whole project of the civilisation, its whole, "noble" purpose. Yet, for most of the history of elitism, these codes were arcane, secondary to the main task of maintaining power. Under Communism, however, which in a certain sense can, with Nazism, be considered the ultimate deterioration of civilisation into madness—the final result of the sickness untreated—under this "institutionalised revolutionism," all other pretenses to class superiority were winnowed away, all *except* this most fundamental one. The *Republic* of Plato justified the horrors of class society by glorying in the abstract thinking the upper class was thus free to engage in. In the Communist world, abstract thinking was not the justification for the horrors of class society – rather, it was the very *reason* for the class society, and all its horrors could be justified as the "inevitability of history" — an abstraction, among others, that the Communists used to set themselves atop the hierarchy. Plato's Citizen Philosopher needed slaves to do the work; Lenin's Professional Revolutionary was needed *by* the slaves to do *his* "work." And his "work" (which was of course his way of avoiding any actual work) was nothing but the naked task of administration itself.

As societies have "evolved" away from animal existence, they have become more distant from the emotional and sensual realities we share with the animals. My own madness has certainly followed the same "evolution." From the warmth of intimate connection to others and the feeling of love for them and myself, to the distancing of my mind away from my body and other people's bodies, into a place of pure abstraction, divorced from palpable reality. Here is where my voices are located—always "out the window," "outside the door," away from the room I'm in and the people I'm with, somehow coldly watching me, judging me. Society's evolution from sensory reality into the realm of equations can be seen as a deterioration into madness—and its result becomes more horrible the more intellectual and ideological its ethos becomes. In a sense, bureaucratic collectivism — totalitarianism — is

An Ethics of Sanity

the most "human" of systems, if we take the civilised definition of what "human" means. Of course, as we've become more human, more separate from animals, more abstract, our societies have degenerated into the worst inhumanity, creating ways of life so nightmarish as to exceed even the most horrific visions of our darkest myths. Economies literally based on burning people alive in ovens have been visited by our species to maintain ourselves in our civilisation — a means by which such economies escaped the Global Depression that was sinking the economies of all their neighbouring nation-states. And in the most wealthy nation in the world today, the United States, one of the only true "growth industries" is the prison-industrial complex. Is such a difference of essence, or merely of degree?

Abstraction allows us to deal with living in the world. But it locks us into the terms we use, and isolates us from the flesh-and-blood reality the terms but represent. Abstraction can be seen as a tool we use to make reality ascertainable, a way to reduce the incomprehensible wealth of stimuli that is the world into patterns we can more easily predict and understand. But in trying to "understand" reality, to hold it, to analyse and dissect it, we distance ourselves from it, distort it, simplify it, and reduce it to an image which is not reality, but rather a picture that we (and, more to the point, our society) demands that it is. It is evident that abstract thinking is historical to our species, that it evolved over time, that other animals do not display the signs of such distancing from their present moment as we have learned to do. Animal life, like plant life, is mostly not divorced from its surroundings the way human life is.

The ability (and the addiction) to reflect, to symbolise, is that which apparently distinguishes our species from the rest. All art, all literature, all science, all mathematics, most all philosophy and religion reflect this reflection, mostly glorying in it, but in any case originating in the tendency.

Abstraction may well be a great "gift" of humanity, and its furtherance and reification is the hallmark of civilisation. But what has it done? It has enabled us to stand apart from the rest of life, and from one another, allowing us to observe, to study. But it has caused this distancing, of dubious merit even when seen neutrally, to become a manifestly harmful and potentially suicidal policy for our species. To distance our species from the rest, to consider the environment as if we lived independently of it and were not in fact inextricably bound up in its totality, has allowed us to quantify and commodify and eventually destroy it. And, even if we are able sustain the fiction that we are separate from it, its fate and ours *are* linked - an inconvenient but damning reality - as we are becoming forced by the changing climate and the depletion of resources finally to admit.

When I was involved in the revolutionary communist group before my crack-up, we relished this abstraction, relished our role as "professional revolutionaries" capable of observing and analysing the problems around us, and (eventually) even the people around us. I find it not coincidental that my madness involves myself being observed and analysed by my voices, in a way like my father's madness had "the bourgeoisie" observing and analysing him, but too, the way we communists observed and analysed everyone else. Observation, the delusion of being separate and thus being able to control the things one observes, is a standpoint embraced by both those who seek to maintain that society, and many of those who wish to replace it. Observation, "impartial" and "dispassionate," is at the core of the outlook of science, the most privileged of all abstract schools of thought in a technological society. To observe, furthermore, is a goal in itself, something which creates identity - a negative identity - in opposition to the observed. And though a doctor might help a patient by examining him, and a viewer of pornography might gain a measure of sexual release from using images of people he doesn't know, and a Napoleon might reorder society for the "betterment" of his subjects by observing the social problem and imposing his Napoleonic Code upon it, none of these people can truly interact with those they observe while in the process of observing them. Thus, the doctor cannot truly understand the sickness of her patient in the same way her patient does (a problem particularly egregious in the case of contemporary psychiatry); thus the viewer of pornography sacrifices intimacy, creativity, and eventually even autonomy when colonised by images which substitute for actual flesh-and-blood people, images selected and designed to induce conformity to an unquestioned beauty standard; thus Napoleon dies alone on his Elba having "liberated" no one, having no friends or human connection with the vast empire of faceless followers that were once his countrymen.

      In science, philosophy, literature, and the arts, we see again and again "the great man" who dissects and analyses not the person or group he studies, but the image of that person or group which already exists in the text of his society. He cannot be impartial. The very nature of his distance from his subject means he cannot know his subject. There are assumptions that come from the very school of thought he operates in, that distort his subject into some abstraction more real for him than any reality he can touch. And his distance prevents him from the possibility of dispelling his prejudices, armed with the arrogance of past "knowledge" of the subject in which his studies are inevitably framed. Thus, he does not question whether man is "the thinking animal"; rather, he assumes that is what he is, and he then looks for reasons by which to justify the assumption. Thus, the "science" of phrenology justified pre-existing Victorian prejudices about race and class and sex, providing scientific terminology and scientific mystique to the already well-accepted "degeneracy" of nonwhites, criminals, radicals, and women. Thus the contemporary pathologizing of non-normative sexualities found in the current and upcoming editions of the Diagnostic-Statistical Manual—which considered homosexuality a "disease" until 1974—and to this day considers trans-identified individuals, most kinky or otherwise sexually-diverse people and behaviours, and many other folk and their practises "sick" and subject to drugging and other forced treatments. Non-normative populations have been and continue to be "scientifically" discriminated against; but what is this but simple prejudice for those unlike the mainstream? - and science simply the latest method of false logic to justify the prejudice, the hatred?

For many centuries, women were prevented from occupying the role of "observer," leading not only to sexist, self-fulfilling perceptions of women in scientific studies and works of art, but to the conclusion based on the "common sense" of the time that women simply did not have the capacity to observe in the same way men did. The same holds true for views of working class and poor people, who may be condemned or even "championed" by members of the elite, but are rarely given the opportunity to speak for themselves. And the culture of "white" society continues to pervert the reality of non-white people by offering images constructed and observed by white outsiders. Be it the white beat cop preying on a black neighbourhood by the very nature of his job as policeman, or the highest centre of academic learning in the United States not fifteen years ago concluding "scientifically" black inferiority to whites based on "impartial" I.Q. tests (written and administered by whites), the outsider-ness of the observer makes it nearly impossible to gain a true understanding of his subject, even with the best of intentions.

The observer is the one whose reality cannot be questioned—except perhaps by other observers, who "observe" and judge him and his work in turn. His reality is assumed to be right and truthful - in fact, it is he who defines not only what is right and truthful, but the very standards which we call "right" and "truth." This assumption comes from the sacred place our civilisation has long given to the intellectual, to the philosopher, to the scientist, to the artist - to the "abstract" thinker. Even those who in their observation conclude society is problematic or unjust, and even advocate radical action against it, remain privileged in their ability to "stand apart" from the society they are viewing. Thus, even the most committed intellectual apologist for capitalism will often concede the value of a Marx; for Marx, despite his revolutionary conclusions, arrived at those conclusions by the methods long hallowed by civilisation. He used "science," he used "philosophy," he used "history" and even "mathematics." And he packaged his critique in terms of his command of written language, the very sign of abstract thought, the greatest currency of civilised discourse. Thus he "deserves" the respect always given to the intellectual, despite his shortcomings and errors, and the shortcomings and errors of those who followed him.

My point here is not to disparage Marx; nor is it to praise him. It is rather to show how unquestioned privilege can duplicate all the worst of class society, even in the attempts of people to throw off the yoke of hierarchy. Those who followed Marx uncritically in the past set up only what could be expected, given the unquestioned elitism in their scientific approach. Their science had proven their need to lead the masses, to organise them, and eventually to police them. This madness, though, is simply a more advanced, chronic state of the madness that has been with us all along.

Of course, capitalism and communism were never purely separate entities. Indeed, they were developments of one another, dependent on one another, *needed* each other to continue to oppress the same global proletariat and peasantry.

During the decades of the Cold War, the rival systems came to resemble each other more and more, the communist empire engaging in economic, "state capitalist" imperialism of its satellites, the capitalist empire employing more and more bureaucracy and techniques of mind control to perpetuate itself. And this is at the heart of the issue: contrary to bourgeois, Marxist, and much "common sense" of people who entertain the notion of "the lesser of two evils" - no form of class society is "progressive." None is any better than any other. All depend on the same lie. My voices represent themselves to me as "bourgeois," as rulers of the rich man's world. This is undoubtedly because I grew up on my father's stories of being persecuted by corporations, and his paranoia was intensified every time our family's economic base was threatened. But the voices' basic ethos is much older than capitalism; their "game" has its roots in the very oldest courtly intrigues of the first Pharaohs (so they've implied). And while other oppressions come up for discussion in my fight with them, it is this reality, that of pure power, that informs all else.

Go to the opera, they exhorted me early on, and look at what is depicted above the bar downstairs from the Lyric Opera lobby in my home in Chicago. There, gilded figures enact the age-old chase: Persephone, running from a satyr-like Hades. *Rape*. This is what the "highest" art form of the most powerful and "advanced" civilisation enshrines. This is the most naked and basic depiction of the dance of this culture. This is the only reality. Winston Smith being tortured by O'Brien, pleading for a world not based in hate. The answer: Power is not a means, but an end; Power is making people suffer; Power is pulling human minds apart, and putting them back together in shapes of one's own choosing. Rape is the perversion of the most intimate and joyful experience a person can have - communion with another. And metaphorically, it is the relationship the dominator has always had with the dominated, throughout time. Ploughing the ground is raping the earth; building obelisks into the air is raping the sky; the postmodern media infusion of information into people's head space is technology raping the human spirit, destroying all that is beautiful in subjectivity - and then forcing people to live on, without dignity, allowing them not even the respite of death.

The same avenues to madness—isolation, abstraction, magical thinking—that led me into my psychosis, are the same paths that have led the human species all along the odyssey from Gilgamesh to Pol Pot. The way my mind fell into madness, the evil I've experienced intimately, is only the ultimate result of the system of power and privilege that has been evolving for millennia, that is now threatening to exterminate the entire human race and all living things rather than abandon its sickness. If the ruling circles had the power, the power of psychic, telepathic control over human minds my voices tell me they do, then I would not be at all surprised if they would indeed concoct such a "game" as the voices have played with me for the last thirteen years, one that I'm destined to be caught up in for the rest of my life. Looking at the past centuries, the powerful have raped the world and its people far more horrendously than any psychosis could torture me.

My psychosis is only a literalisation of the pressures inherent in the society all around us, just one small example of what a person dealing with such a world can be driven to invent to reflect an insane reality.

Psychosis is world culture's ultimate end, on the personal as well as the global level. Whether it is the ever-increasing number of schizophrenic, depressive, and other "crack ups" in the population as society decays, or the "sane" pursuits of entire economies based on the development and marketing of pesticides and prisons and weapons of mass destruction (so reminiscent of the equally profitable marketing of Zyklon-B and crematoria but a generation or two in the past) to continue this wretched way of life, psychoses such as mine will not be aberrations from the norm, but the very destiny of civilised humanity.

      The voices my unconscious has created to reflect my world worship hate as the only real strength. They implore me to "look down" on them with contempt. (They promise to leave me in peace if I do.) But to compromise here would be worse than being tortured by them. For the concept of "superiority" is foreign to my most basic, gut-level sense of myself. Moreover, it is foreign to any truly liberatory ethics. To oppose violence, sometimes one must have recourse to violence. But to rape is to surrender to the hate of one's oppressor, to become the evil one sought to oppose. It is possible to kill another without seeing them as inferior. In the combat of the Samurai, or the Knights of old Europe, or the wars waged by tribal peoples throughout the world, the enemy could be an honoured enemy, the battle not based in hate but in sacred duty. The hunter-gatherer tribes of the present and the past do not have contempt for their prey; rather, they thank them, do rituals to appease their spirits, even worship them as their moral superiors. The Neanderthal peoples were known to have built tombs not only for themselves, but for the cave bears they hunted. The relationship of killing to dehumanisation and contempt is not a fixed one. It can be performed with hate, surely, but hate is not necessary for its existence.

An Ethics of Sanity

But rape must dehumanise to exist - both the rapist and the victim. It is an act worse than murder; for there is no possibility of beauty, honour, or vision in it. It is the ultimate manifestation of power, power's naked meaning. Civilisation claims its laws and customs facilitate the necessary means of protection of the weak from the strong, the suppression of the "natural," ugly desires which we are told are at our base, in order to foster a "better" humanity, who "evolves" from brutishness to refinement. The basic ugliness of the untrained, unrefined human animal has been the essential justification for all systems of hierarchy since their inception, and the urge to "rising" into civilisation is the ascending from the dirt and want of aboriginal existence to the airy, heady summit of the ziggurat. But rape in its actual and metaphoric realities has always been part of conquest, its institutionalisation an indispensable part of the way the world sustains itself. The rape of Persephone is the denial of Demeter; the rape of the Sabines the genesis of Rome. Rape is not prevented by civilisation; it is *caused* by civilisation. Rape is the ultimate civilised act.

All forms of privilege arise from delusion, and perpetuate delusion. The delusion is based in distance, in separateness, and from there goes into superiority and contempt. We come to relate to others as if they were separate from us fundamentally, ignoring that the actions of one always affect the reality of another. The very air we breathe is breathed by others. The degradation of one paves the way for the potential degrading of all. No being can be separate from the environment around it, but like it or not is part of the community of life. This is not a mystical or sentimental statement. This is hard reality, as our species is finding out the hard way. Separation exists only as an abstraction, and it makes use of abstraction to continue. The pursuit of separation leads to dissociation, the state where I myself and all of you will eventually find madness - psychic pain, and lack of love. And within ourselves, separation of rational from emotional, spiritual from physical, right from left - all of it eventually leads to self-loathing and anhedonia - the ingredients for schizophrenic crack-up. Whether this crack-up occurs in the manifestation of diagnosable "symptoms," or whether it leads to the quiet desperation of consumerist "sane" normality, or if it encourages membership in some fascistic cult - *it will have an effect on you.* And what is often the result is the clinging to privilege, the perpetuation of the fiction of isolation, fear, and paranoia - and the decision to rape another, the only way to reach out to another when abstraction has poisoned oneself and one's reality, till nothing has meaning any more.

But both in the world and in myself, I have found it is possible to heal. An ethics of sanity must proceed from describing the symptoms and delusions of personal and social psychosis to providing suggestions for their treatment and cure. Proceeding thus, we come to the spiritual, psychological, and social potentials for healing and wholeness.

An Ethics of Sanity

Chapter IV: Healing the Schism

Now we come to an ethics of sanity. Having seen the problem, the isolated, unfeeling dissociation every one of us struggles against in order to find beauty in our human relations, that which ruins our attempts at autonomy and denies our connection with others struggling with the same forces, we proceed to the means by which we can attain wholeness once again. To oppose privilege, we must understand the roots of the desire for privilege, and thus make an effort to extricate ourselves from our cultural conditioning, forfeit the enticing but ultimately dehumanising attraction to seeing ourselves as "better" than our fellow human beings, affirming in its stead the much greater and more fulfilling path to loving ourselves as we truly are - flawed and imperfect, but in that whole and real. This path is the path of sanity, and it cannot be completed without loving - not only ourselves, but all human beings in the greater community of resistance to the global civilisation, which attempts to instill paranoia and hatred in others and ourselves, even as we struggle to find a meaning for our lives.

I am limited, very, very limited, by the words I use to convey this vision. In words is the unacknowledged but damning servility to the empire of abstraction. Thus, I can never in words hope to express the experience of rapture, of connection, of *pure love* which transcends all paradigms and allows us to see a vision which we all sense is possible - a world without power, without privilege, without slavery to the hierarchy of convenience, that path of willful ignorance to the atrocities daily committed to keep this civilisation running. The "cure" to the schizophrenia at the heart of our culture, or at the very least a "treatment" aimed at fostering its cure, is to reverse the trend towards isolation and distrust underlying all we think of as "normal" in dealing with our fellow human beings, with the wider world of nature, and the domination of inhuman, unnatural institutions whose power causes the momentum we've known as "progress" to the fate awaiting us if this culture proceeds to its logical, insane conclusion. We must reject the isolation at the heart of delusion, and experience one another as we truly are - infinite, the source of health and happiness, the miracle which has kept our species going through all the dark nights of this civilised existence.

The above outline of three primary delusions, that of the masculine, the white, and the elitist, is by no means exhaustive. But within these delusions can be ascertained much of the human dilemma. I would like to do more than deconstruct them in the following pages; I would like to suggest possible ways to transcend them, based on the ways I have transcended them personally, have seen others transcend them, and have learned from still others through their writing, art, music, and studies how these abstractions can be abandoned, and a more whole humanity can be embraced.

Masculinity, that abstraction which is so taken for granted by our culture - and by those "males" who are cajoled into identifying with it - is isolation, is dissociation, is madness. The path to personal and social healing involves its radical rejection and disavowal. What will this mean in practical terms? The masculine dream, that nightmare of abbreviated humanity offered to half our species in compensation for the pain of realising it, has much to do with what is "normative" in the rest of the species. Its definition comes from the larger conception of sex roles of which it is master; and these sex roles and the mindset which "purifies" it, excluding all who go against its assumptions, collectively function as straight sexuality. It is here that I'd like to begin to trace the possibilities for

An Ethics of Sanity

healing.

Queerness as Liberation from Straightness

As with all other categories, the terms "straight" and "queer" are abstractions. They are approximations of reality, rather than reality itself; and thus, they are understood differently by the different people who use them. For some, "straight" denotes simply the orientation of heterosexuality, and is seen as a basic essentialism. In this view, "queer" denotes its opposite, and pertains to those oriented toward other sexualities than heterosexual ones. Queer, then, is also an essentialism, and as an essentialism - not a choice - it has come to be tolerated as something a minority of people "can't help" being.

My use of these terms are not these essentialist denotations. Rather, like "white" and "black," or "masculine" and "feminine," they are indicative of a *choice* - a way of understanding how something essential in one's physical makeup is socially connoted into a status. More is made of these supposedly "essential" things than need be made of them. Though one cannot help being seen and judged by others according to superficially apparent signs, like pale skin or facial hair for instance, one *does* have a choice as to how one as an individual will relate to others and to oneself in the light of these things. Male, female, as well as other (cf. inter-sexual), may indeed exist as essentials of biology. But it is a big leap to assume about others and oneself that these biologically essential aspects of one's identity must necessarily carry over into the coded kinds of behaviour and power-relations that "masculinity" and "femininity"- i.e. gender roles, as opposed to incidental sex characteristics - mandate in our society. Similarly, "whiteness" is only incidentally connected to the melanin content of one's skin; white is something connotative, by which denotative, essential realities become more broadly construed into a social reality. Straightness, then, is not so much about heterosexuality *per se* as about how that orientation is made "normative" within the society. In making it normative, society limits sexual expression, not only for those defined outside the norm, but also for those defining themselves within it. There is in straightness a kind of duty imposed to stay within the norm, and in order to "be straight," a person is expected to *stay straight*. Queerness is by its very definition thus akin to *perversion*; and the vast realm of possibility for sexual experience which goes outside the heteronormative strictures must be condemned, or at the very least personally avoided by straight people, or else the "sinful" and the "sick" will "pervert" them.

Queerness, as opposed to "gayness" (which denotes and connotes a stable minority status rather than a mindset), connotes sexual freedom and adventurousness, the willingness to experiment, and ultimately to find one's own peculiar preferences as part of a uniquely individual identity. Queerness involves a willingness to go deeper into one's own and one's lovers' sexuality than the "normal" straight standards could ever allow, to push beyond one's apparent limits into "edge-play," daring to explore the frontiers of one's comfort-zone for the sheer joy of the exploration. Queerness does not pertain to some essential minority status; rather, it is something open to *all sexualities and orientations*. It constitutes a challenge to the very notion of sexual essentialism. Queerness does not seek to simply "live-and-let-live" in a society based on sexual repression. Rather, Queerness seeks to challenge *all people* to question that repression, affirming in its stead individual freedom and encouraging the boundless sexual potential of everyone, heterosexual, homosexual, bisexual, transgender, sadomasochist, and all others *ad infinitum*.

Just as heterosexual people can therefore be queer, if they seek true self-exploration and autonomy from the normative strictures of society, so can non-heterosexual people act straight, limiting the expression and variety of their sexual experience, remaining "pure" of "deviancies" by policing their fantasies, and accepting a narrow beauty standard. This was a prime reason for the old divide between what was called the "Gay Movement" and the "Queer Movement" in the 1990s. Not only was the difference about the level of inclusiveness, with Queer open to all sexual minorities rather than excluding all not "homo-normative" and assimilationist, but more to the point it was about the whole attitude toward sexuality in general as imposed by society's Straight value-system.

Gay is an attitude that seeks to live within the society without challenging it. It does this primarily by arguing for the essentialism of orientation, demanding from society not the radical rethinking of its sexual mores, but merely to coexist with them as a "slightly different" kind of straight. "We can't help being who we are," is what the Gay (Straight) mindset says to the larger society, and therefore "please, leave us be." Queer, on the other hand, is all about affirming *choice* in matters of sexuality, and is therefore far more threatening to the institution of Straightness - as well as all the rest of authoritarian society. By rejecting essentialism and affirming choice in terms of gender, behaviour, and relationships, Queerness poses the challenge to everyone to rethink what makes them the way they are, as well as embracing all manner of "perversities" as positive goods in the formation of an independent, nonconformist, and above all *joyful* attitude toward sexuality. This flies in the face of the grim, anhedonic normality by which civilisation denies people a prime source of transcendence and connection.

An Ethics of Sanity

The conventional wisdom of society, even among those who oppose the uglier aspects of homophobia and strive to be tolerant, is that queer sex is an aberration, something outside "normal" sex. It is seen as anti-biological, and therefore not as "natural" as heterosexuality. But this misconstrues what sex is for. In the animal kingdom, as well as amongst human beings, sexual relations only sometimes involve reproduction. Heterosexual or not, the majority of sexual acts among creatures do not always or even often produce pregnancy and lead to birth. Rather, they serve as bonding, as pleasure, as the mediation of social tensions, and many other things.

The product-oriented mindset with sex fits well with capitalism, and surely stems from the original "be fruitful and multiply" directive of the early civilised god to its male and female human worshipers, who were commanded to populate the earth with children of their own nation in order to subdue the earth (and other nations). Focusing on the mechanical "function" of sex is part and parcel of the strained relations between the genders, who are expected to "produce" offspring. Any other kind of sexual contact is relegated then to something "lower" than "real" sex, and comes to be regarded as strange, "dirty," "sick," "sinful"- or at the very least, less than satisfying. Straight people tend to see non-productive sex as "foreplay," something done to "get ready" for the "real thing." This is if they acknowledge it at all. And, by buying into the idea that sex is "for" production, that production is its "real" purpose, it then becomes possible to diminish its potential significance, limiting not only the act itself, but the very joy of contact which a wider range and freedom of activities would unleash.

Straightness ties into the gender role fixation quite well, as well as all the mutual dissatisfaction at the heart of the masculine and feminine mindsets. Straight sex defines masculine and feminine, and the assumption that it is "natural" and "all there is" dialectically reinforces the assumption of the "naturalness" of the sex roles. Isolation with inexpressible pain, doubt, and distrust of the other is the sad lot in life of most straight people, "male" or "female," "heterosexual" or "gay." Sex as seen as mechanical, a mere function of biological necessity, can be stripped of most of its wonder, and also distanced from the rest of living.

If sex is something one only does with one's partner, who is strange and other even at the best of times, and one is already a stranger to one's own otherness - the man suppressing his own "woman-ness," and the woman suppressing her own "man-ness," making it very hard to fulfill a partner with whom one by definition has no kinship - sex is "an occasion" rather than the rule, and is compartmentalised into a "holiday" from the rest of reality. This reality - most of our day-to-day living - is almost defined as being not sensuous, not "fun," not wondrous - as the few encounters of the sexual are desperately hoped to be. Sex becomes obsessive precisely because of its distance from a desensualised normality. Further, its status as an "event" makes the pressure to "perform" in it akin to yet another kind of "work," draining even what little wonder is allowed by such a culture to exist in it. Pressure, guilt, fear of failure - all of this gets mixed up into sex. And with the alienated otherness of the partner making it nearly impossible to really know him or her, or experience sexuality as he or she experiences it, what other result is really likely other than failure?

Stuck with isolation, and with the inevitable dissatisfaction that follows from it, a person begins to cling to any privilege or power one can wield against a partner whom one resents for not fulfilling him or her in the way that a freer sexual life might offer. The straight man and woman does not blame straightness for the prison of their relationship, or the alienation that makes them strangers and even competitors in the bedroom, but the partner. The instability of relationships, the inability to find happiness within them, is an endemic and epidemic crisis in straight society today. But few people seem to realise that it is exactly sexual immaturity, the discomfort with the self and the other, and the unwillingness to explore sexuality as a realm of vast potential instead of a packaged commodity, a little "thing" to be got and used - that is to blame for so much of the loneliness and unhappiness in our culture.

Queerness of course does not in itself guarantee happiness. But it is geared toward a greater potential for fulfillment, precisely because it mandates a greater amount of exploration than simply accepting the straight norms. Most queer people have had to "come out" to themselves and others. By coming out to yourself, you are forced to know yourself better than you once did. Even if the questioning is answered rather quickly, still the questions get asked. In order to accept yourself, you must affirm your basic goodness and beauty in spite (and because) of your difference from straight society. Straight people do not have to "come out" about being straight. Therefore, the impetus - the *requirement* - to grow just isn't there. The degree to which heterosexual people do find fulfillment, sexual maturity, and are willing to explore themselves without fear of "perversion," is the degree to which they deviate from straightness. Such things as slavery to the beauty standard, the commodification of the other, the fear of one's own or one's partner's "kinkiness," the suppression within oneself of any sexual otherness, the willingness to confine oneself strictly into the gender category one was born and/or socialised into even if one cannot fit comfortably into it - along with all the privileges society grants to those who exhibit these self-policing conformities - are things indicative of straightness. They must be rejected if one is to achieve autonomy. Sexual autonomy, like any other form of autonomy, is both an end and a means to an end. That end is freedom from the society of oppression; and through individual freedom, the way becomes clear for activism within a community of resistance, designed to achieve social emancipation from the centuries of the civilised delusion.

Sexual health and freedom begins with an experience, impossible to put into words, of one's own beauty. This means appreciation of one's desirability, "owning" one's sexuality by forming a self-image unaffected by society's narrow standards of beauty. Crucial to this is the regular practicing of self-love in the form of exploring one's body, emotions, fantasies, etc., and learning to experience and enjoy autonomy and self-fulfillment. This by nature is a revolutionary act. It goes against all the paranoia of society's sexual relations, because it makes one independent of the compulsion to use others to gratify some narrow "need"- the essentially cynical and ugly utilitarianism which society offers to belittle the sexuality which in other eras it sought to drive completely underground. Now somewhat "out of the closet" because of the partially successful Sexual Revolution of the 1960s and 70s, sexuality must be penned into the most abbreviated and stunted expressions possible if society is still to exercise control. Sexuality must, if hierarchy is to continue, be made as little satisfying as it can be made to be; thus "straightness."

Basic to the whole suppression of sexuality - and this goes for all orientations - is the denial of the beauty of the individual, the robbing of the birthright to sexual transcendence and ecstasy. People who experience sexual pleasure regularly, as well as all the other aspects of bonding and love, are less willing to sacrifice their lives to the routines of labour or the brutality of war. This is the reason every repressive society has made the policing of sex a priority. Separation from sexual happiness makes life feel cheaper, less meaningful, and therefore easier to throw away to the needs of the power structure. Also, the schism within relates to all other schisms, the delusional mindset at the heart of all privilege, the denial of human beauty leading to cynicism and contempt and eventually the acceptance and exercise of cruelty. To rob a person of his or her sexual joy is an essential prerequisite to the whole project of getting him or her to be distant from everything else.

Civilisation could not continue without this basic impoverishment, making its citizens beg for whatever crumbs are cast off the master's table, fighting ravenously against each other for the tiniest scraps. It is no coincidence that at the final stages of a civilisation, be it Rome or Weimar or the present moment, faith in sexual mores is lost. Freedom in the sexual can hasten the fall of empires. And while a conservative defender of the system might bewail its coming, the fall of empire is necessary to any realisation of emancipation.

Self-love, and self-exploration, are at the core of sexual health. The Victorian prohibition on masturbation, invoking "scientific" connections to madness, follows from the purely religious aversion to it going back to Biblical times. Masturbation was seen as the most cardinal of all sins by the Catholic Church until very recent times, worse even than homosexuality, and far worse than heterosexual sex before marriage. Why this fear throughout history? Because masturbation is the ultimate affirmation of self-hood - and this is the number one enemy of despotism. Self-love is freedom, from the society of repression, and from over-dependence on others. In freedom from over-dependence on others, the possibility exists for more fulfilling relations with others. The self-lover knows herself and can communicate what she's discovered with her other lovers. And, emancipated from the urge to use her other lovers, she both defies their unnatural power over her, and her own temptation to claim power over them. Love becomes more a matter of choice than need. And a relationship based on choice is the only one which is healthy and free.

When a person gets to know herself intimately, she is less a mystery to herself, and what mystery remains becomes not a fearful abyss of uncertainty and doubt, but a beckoning frontier into which she journeys with a sense of adventure. There, deep within herself, is a beauty which has yet to be actualised, to be known - and discovering it and appreciating it can be a source of strength for all other revolutionary endeavor. More concretely and practically, the unconscious, whose fantasies well up into consciousness during self-loving exploration, is the wellspring of much of the hidden, underlying motivations for a person's behaviour. Knowing it more intimately is a key to emancipating oneself from slavery to the patterns one finds oneself stuck in without knowing why. This process can help free a person from acting in selfish, unkind ways - something which allows him or her to be a better revolutionary, a more giving, capable member of a community of resistance.

Every occasion of masturbatory exploration offers a chance to try out new roles, explore new ways to get turned on, as well as revisit - and thus more deeply understand - all the older ones. Most people raised in civilised society fail to value these occasions for the precious opportunities they are. Self-love is denigrated, devalued, covered in shame. It is at best seen as utilitarian, a poor substitute for "real" sex, a "quick-fix" to satisfy some "urge"; more often, it is equated with desperation, even failure, because what

An Ethics of Sanity

one *should* be doing is engaging in sex with a partner, preferably a partner of the opposite gender for the purpose of making babies. Yet, intimacy with the self is not selfish, but a key way to avoid selfishness. All the many, many things one might conceive in fantasy can be realised without regard to social strictures or fear of harming or being harmed by others. In the safe space of one's own mind, one can try out anything - and it behooves the self-adventurer to allow the unconscious to suggest scenarios as far out as possible, even things that seem strange or even frightening, things one would never do in reality. These safe times are opportunities to go out to the very limits of what can be conceived; and the beautiful thing about it is that, once a session is over, you can hold onto all you've learned, and not affect the outside world one iota.

Self-love at the base of the free person's sexuality leads to true love of others. True love, which is selfless, and giving, and valuing of the other. Love, mature and powerful, is the revolutionary attitude, the very basis for any ethics of sanity. Hatred and fear, paranoia and distrust - these things make society go, and without them hierarchy cannot sustain itself. It is the poverty of the individual, his hatred and fear of himself, which leads to his clinging to privilege and power over others. Resentment is a key component of homophobia as well as sexism. Queer people often seem to have a greater sense of their own beauty than what is thought "natural" or "right" for the mainstream to have; they seem "prettier" than they should be, paying more attention to how they look and why they choose to look that way.

This basic regard for themselves as beautiful smacks of a kind of elitism to many, something "better" than the straight people—particularly straight men, who consciously and unconsciously view themselves as inherently ugly. Women in straight society are often resented for the same reasons as queer folk on this score; there is something "proud" about them, and it is this pride which misogynists wish to bring down. It is this hatred of the beautiful which fuels much of the rape and the queer-bashing and all the subtler means of punishing those who dare not to feel as miserable and ugly as civilisation says we all should feel.

I went through a period of isolation following my crisis which lasted for nearly eight years. My relationship which had survived the terrors of the crisis, the difficult times where I was paranoid of even close friends, shouted at walls and had long, heated arguments with the voices walking down the street, my lover sticking with me through all of it—this relationship did not survive the year after it. During that time, I became so deadened by anti-hallucinogens I could no longer function in any way sexually, and lost interest in sex with my partner. I do not blame her for leaving me, though at the time it was very hard. I slid into further isolation after that, not having a significant love-relationship again for the next seven-and-a-half years. I can trace my further degeneration into psychosis and general ill health to this. On the bright side, I've found my health has increased exponentially over the last several years when I reconnected to two old lovers, and then met the love of my life, my current partner. It seems an absurd thing to me to hear that there was actually a scientific study conducted recently which concluded that schizophrenics might actually benefit from love-relationships (as if such a thing would need such a study to be understood as obvious!). Reconnection with my physicality, my sensuality, and sharing emotional intimacy has, more than any other single factor, been integral to rescuing my soul from the abstracted prison of my mind.

The voices have, like the society they manifest, always attempted to disrupt and denigrate my sexuality.

An Ethics of Sanity

They always try to insinuate themselves into my sexual experiences, whether alone or with partners. They are *jealous* of the freedom I can achieve from them by losing myself in the warm realm of sexual transcendence. As I've come to greater health over the years, and even during the depths of my crisis thirteen years ago, I found that of the many "boxes" they tried to put me in ("worker," "revolutionary," "theist," "atheist," "artist," "white," "intellectual," "man"), their enticements to be "straight" has been one of their most passionate pursuits.

There was a point during my relationship whilst in the depths of my crisis where I felt very sexually boxed in, with all the ugliness and self-hatred and inadequacy of being a "man," unable to please my lover, or myself. Shortly after, though, as if in answer to a desperate prayer, I had an experience with my lover in which I dressed in drag—something I hadn't done since before I'd been a communist, years and years before. I found my lover (who was female-bodied) appreciated how I looked, and found her own queerness in response, becoming masculine to suit my femininity. Even the voices had to stand in awe of the power I was able to attain against them when dressed in this triumphantly beautiful way.

Only months ago, my queerness served me again against the voices. They were whispering hatreds at me, as always they do, when they got on the tangent of raping me, describing it in the most horrifying and frightening ways. For some reason, instead of fighting against this and falling into their "man vs. man" trap, I *embraced* the fears, and transformed the experience of their raping me into a masochistic fantasy. I "got off" on their threats and their images, and forced them thus to serve *me!* Since that moment a few months ago, they've never threatened me like that again, and in fact have been mostly quieter lately, as my ego has emerged, easily and naturally, from the morass of their ego-dystonia. Sexuality, free, self-chosen, and queer, has been my liberation.

I believe it will continue to be my liberation in the future. One of the art projects I was involved with in the last year was a Radical Queer Pornography collective called "Glamarchy." One of the films I'd like to make with them (though at the point of this writing, it remains but an idea) is a "Schizo-Porn." It would involve a schizophrenic central character being tortured by his/her voices, being abused by them. But at some point, the schizo would rise against them—"flipping" them from the top role to the role of the bottom—and thus triumph. The short piece would be all the fun of S/M and multiple-partner pornography; but it would also be a way to dramitise madness in a way that would show how sexuality and owning it can transform madness into *ecstasy!*

There are many revolutionaries who do not value the sexual aspects of liberation; their appraisal of the human animal is therefore stunted and incomplete. Is it any wonder that such "revolutionaries" build "revolutionary societies" more degraded even than the madness they sought to overthrow? This ties into a whole argument about the way radical people should behave. Those who advocate "seriousness" and "sacrifice" in pursuing radical politics, and argue for a schism between that and "lifestyle" aspects of radicalism, miss the whole point of revolutionary change. Further, they misunderstand the very process of revolution. Such things as "lifestyle" can never be truly separated from "serious" political work. To live for some future event to the detriment of what is lived now is exactly the deferred gratification at the heart of capitalism. Revolution exists in the moment, as well as in the future. Living well, and living free—not only is this necessary for doing "serious" work, but it is *part of this*

An Ethics of Sanity

work. Liberated people gain maturity, and this allows them to be more loving towards their fellows, more giving, and less inclined to dominate and claim unconscious (or conscious) privilege in dealing with politics, or anything else. Marx said the society of today is "pregnant" with the society of tomorrow—and he was right. Revolutionary living *is* revolution. The process of emancipation must begin immediately.

Living in emancipation gives radicals the psychic strength to endure the ordeals awaiting them in the future, to build from their consciousness and the consciousness of their communities of resistance a way of living which expands into the whole of the decaying society. An alternative must be offered to what exists, and clearly that alternative must be one of deed as well as stated belief. It is attractive - and thus a potentially persuasive model - only to the degree that it fulfills the needs and desires of those who make with their lives a defiance of the hatred and paranoia that fuels society's madness.

A queer attitude toward sexuality, and from that to relationships, is an offering of sanity against the forces of an insane society. To accept straightness in one's life is to give up not only one's individual birthright to exploration and self-love; it is to founder in the quest to emancipate oneself from the institutionalised immaturity and resulting selfishness that is key to maintaining the current social order. Sexual freedom is not "on the side" of other issues of radicalism; nor, of course, is it in itself the total picture. But without it, defying a society of hate becomes most difficult. And as we are all flawed beings, the quest for maturity becomes self-evidently important in overcoming our inadequacies and developing the ability to stand against privilege - something tempting even to the best of us - and something, too, which nearly everyone, regardless of their social category, can be guilty of indulging.

Liberation from Whiteness

The pain and paranoia of straightness leads directly to the contempt of sexism, to the "battle of the sexes" which neither of the "essential" genders can win, and to homophobia and all the related hatreds of "perverse" people. The delusion of whiteness is based in similar patterns of paranoia and distrust of others and the self. Like the first complex of delusions, whiteness, too, must ultimately be rejected if one is to free not only the "other races," but the Caucasians who cling to a privileged status that causes them to side against their potential allies and acquiesce to a system only marginally more their friend. A good deal of the fear expressed by Caucasians in recent years of "reverse racism" stems from a cynical understanding of humanity, and an ignorance to history which has proven time and time again the liberating drive of nonwhite expressions of identity for *all races*. It is this cynicism and this ignorance which entices people to claim their racial privilege, even if they would rather not do so. Most white people feel they have no choice.

Most people in the world, regardless of race, are at least dimly aware that European peoples have brutalised the planet's people over the course of the last several centuries. Many are aware that through neo-colonialism in the south and institutionalised racism in the northern countries, those who claim predominantly European ancestry continue to dominate and destroy the world. And even those who hate these things will many times feel imprisoned in their pale flesh, and conclude that any future revolutionary upheaval will target them, like it or not, right alongside those more agreeable to the system of racist oppression. This "imprisonment" in whiteness serves to paralyze many Caucasians, leading to a useless "white guilt" which seems the only alternative to virulent white racism. There is a fear that the "darker" peoples will unleash their anger in anti-white "racist" ways, that they will do to the whites all the evil things that have been done to them in exacting their long overdue revenge.

White people who cling to white identity - even when they don't want to cling to it - tend to judge all people by the same standard by which they judge themselves - a very pessimistic standard. White people tend to assume all people operate in a racial continuum based in hate. Therefore they fear "militancy" amongst non-whites as inherently threatening to them, regardless of how far fetched the scenario of white victimisation really is. But the truth about non-white militancy is that, historically, it is most forgiving to whites. And even those non-whites without a great deal of political consciousness or militancy are obviously much more forgiving than it even seems humanly possible. This racist civilisation could not go on a single day without degenerating into outright civil war if it weren't for the constant forgiveness of non-whites for the racism, personal and institutional, of white neighbours, co-workers, bosses, and police.

How often have race riots killed large numbers of whites? Most occurrences of such racial violence over the last century or more have been white people killing blacks, Asians, Indians, etc. - not the other way around. This is simply a historical fact. And when there have been isolated opportunities for true power to be wielded by non-whites over whites (the period of Reconstruction after the American Civil War comes to mind, as does the period following the overthrow of Apartheid in South Africa), people of colour have been amazingly forgiving, willing to work with even their former masters to forge a new and better society. Black militancy, as well as other peoples of colour's militancy, has rarely targeted whites who wish to disavow white racism - in fact in many,

many cases, the hand of comradeship has been extended, and white radicals and people of colour have formed coalitions to fight their common oppressors.

During the Reconstruction, the activists working with the Freedman's Bureau worked to educate and empower poor whites along with blacks. During the Black Power Movement of the 1960s a century later, the Black Panthers formed coalitions like Fred Hampton's Rainbow Coalition, working with both poor whites (i.e. the Young Patriots) as well as more privileged whites (such as in the alliance with the Students for a Democratic Society and the Weather Underground). And when the decades of genocidal racism in South Africa under the Apartheid regime was overthrown, the transition was remarkably peaceful; the Afrikaaner ruling National Party was not outlawed, their adherents not jailed or otherwise persecuted—but allowed to remain as part of the Coalition Government with the African National Congress which it had brutally suppressed just a few years before, and it was then allowed to reorganize as an official Opposition Party to the ANC until just a few years ago, when the party voluntarily dissolved themselves.

Historically, it is not non-white betrayal of white allies, but the reverse that is the rule. The largely-European Communist Party's organising drives in Harlem in the 1930s, as grimly satirised in Ralph Ellison's *Invisible Man*, abandoned black people when it proved inconvenient to stand with them. The radical Knights of Labor in the nineteenth century, those earlier champions of militant working class solidarity in the United States, went out of its way to support the exclusion of Chinese workers, failing to defend them against pogrom-style attacks and supporting restrictions on their immigration. And must we go back to the archetypal American "First Thanksgiving," when the Pilgrims were saved from starvation by Indians - only to murder them soon after in genocidal war?

Even in the most virulent of "counter-racist" responses of people of colour to white people, such as the creation myth expounded by Elijah Muhammad in his *A Message to the Black Man in America*, which explained the white race's genesis as the failed experiment of a "mad scientist" to breed a "devil race," and his belief that it was "too late" for white Christians to accept his brand of Islam and thus be saved - even here, the exhortation was *never* to kill white people, or enslave them, or even drive them from their land. All the early Nation of Islam people wanted was to instill a pride in being black that was a radical rejection of the colonised identity forced on black people by the racist white establishment, and, following the earlier ideas of Marcus Garvey, establish a "Black Nation" independent of white influence. So, the very "worst" that has ever come out of the black community in the country that grew to prominence on their bloodied backs—the most "hateful" viewpoint—was simply the desire for black separation. Never genocide. Never enslavement. Never even race war.

Malcolm X, when founding his own organisation after leaving the Nation of Islam, was asked by a snide white reporter whether any white people would be allowed to join it. His answer: "John Brown - if he was alive." John Brown is a very wonderful figure in the history of race relations. This is because he was among the only "white" men in history to completely give up his white privilege and give his life for the cause of Black Liberation. This shows that even the most militant and suspicious of black activists can allow for the radical rejection of whiteness by sincere white people - even if the possibility seems very slim, the historical examples few and far between. There are the rare white people who fight selflessly for people of colour, and each of them in doing so undergoes a transformation that is seen and respected by even a Malcolm X. They refuse the "honour" of Whiteness, and instead proclaim their *humanity.*

John Brown was not a "white liberal" operating out of a sense of "white guilt." Rather, he was a *human being* determined to help his fellow human beings, to the point of killing those who looked like him to free those who did not. White guilt is only suffered by those who still cling to their white identity, however much they do not like it. They see history as "their" race's injustices against "other people." A human being, regardless of colour, can choose to side with any cause at all. And as a human being, a revolutionary has a *right* to be angry - as angry as anybody else - about the injustice at the heart of civilisation. This anger, rather than guilt, can be a self-affirming motivation for action. Of course, one will always have the particular appearance one was born with. But it is a very big mistake to invest that appearance with any conception of loyalty to a system one feels deeply angry about. And it is an even bigger mistake to assume everyone else in the world thinks according to the same racism that afflicts the dominant caste.

There is prejudice in every community. The way prejudice translates into "racism" is often explained as a dynamic of power. Thus, people of colour do not have the *power* to translate their prejudice against whites into racism. White people's prejudice against non-whites is bolstered by a system much bigger and much older than they themselves are personally. White racism is backed by centuries of institutionalised action and the current power and genocidal policies of the dominant nation-states and the mostly white-run multinational corporations. But I think it necessary to go a step further than this "politically correct" way of viewing it. Anti-white prejudice is not simply not "racist" in the same way white prejudice is—rather, it is the *only sane*

An Ethics of Sanity

response to such a system and a history of atrocity that this civilisation is. It is only *common sense*. And rather than be offended or fearful because of it, the "white" person should really understand that she, too, should hate "whiteness" - as much, if not *more so,* than the people of colour who are displaying the hatred. Anger has its place in radicalism; even hate does. The trick is to see that at all times, it is a *system* which should be hated, that should be the target of anger. When people of colour talk about opposing "the White Man," there is usually no particular white man being spoken of. Rather, the White Man is a symbol of white, patriarchal (and often, capitalist) domination. As white people - that is, people extended the privilege of whiteness, which they can either accept or reject - the decision is always there either to side against whiteness, or by action, word, and thought, to become The White Man. And to feel that there is no choice is to leave yourself no choice.

The plain fact of the matter is that a minority of Caucasians have always lived in communities of colour, and they are mostly accepted as more or less people of colour themselves - unless, of course, they fight the assimilation. How often in white neighborhoods has the same tolerance - let alone assimilation - been offered to non-whites? The paranoia of white communities is notorious - regardless of social class. White neighborhoods are "protected" from non-white outsiders by police, as well as often by organised or spontaneous vigilantism. The phenomenon of demographic change in urban areas tends in both directions, of course. But when white yuppies move into a community of colour, the neighbours are eventually forced to leave because they can't afford to live there any more. When an area changes to non-white people, whites tend to leave much more readily and quickly. The "lowered property values" which racist whites always speak of in connection with such demographic change are not the magical result of a non-white presence, but simply the supply/demand result of so many white people selling their land cheaply in order to get the hell out. Thus, in both cases, it is white racism that affects demographic change. And it is here that the locus of oppression always resides.

White pride is offered to those paralyzed by white guilt as the system's way of maintaining itself. But it is the kind of identity which enslaves its holder to the system of oppression which no one but the most ugly would ever want to defend. Let us recall that "white" identity has never existed in itself; it is always the result of a social engineering designed to force amnesia on those enticed by it. Forgetting one's real origins is necessary for whiteness to be embraced. Along with this amnesia for origins is the amnesia for solidarity, the possibility one's immigrant ancestors had to ally with other peoples not included in the privileged white caste. Whiteness as a political identity is always one manipulated by the system to justify itself. It is thus always reactionary. White pride is merely the other side of the coin of white guilt. Neither of them are real. Each of them assumes the essentialism of what is, after all, but a learned, socially-engineered identity; and thus, it involves choice.

The liberation from the delusion of whiteness involves healing the schism at its root. Paranoia comes from the fear of perceived difference, and the valuing of that difference according to a standard hallowed by society, but which actually has no intrinsic importance. Non-white people have been, and continue to be, the victims of genocidal institutional violence around the world. One does not have to go back a hundred years to slavery or colonialism to find this reality. It is happening right now. Those five-sixths of the world who now starve and slave because of global capitalism are almost all people defined as "non-white." And in Europe

An Ethics of Sanity

and the United States, people of colour are disproportionately imprisoned, discriminated against in areas of housing and employment, are the victims of police harassment and vigilante hate crimes, and are generally made to feel inferior because the dominant language, the cultural icons, and the beauty standard of the civilisation in which they live are all against them, devaluing them, rendering them invisible, attempting to cause their metaphoric and even literal suicide.

Being sensitive to all this will not only allow a "white" person to sympathise with anti-white anger and even hatred. It will cause a crisis of identity that will make the "white" person proud to *deny* whiteness, and bless even the most militant of non-white resistance against a culture and a civilisation with which they no longer identify, nor in any way defend. White pride *and* white guilt presuppose identity with and defense of a social role which countless generations of human beings were not even aware of, and which they at times actively fought against (cf. Bacon's Rebellion, the Rainbow Coalition, etc., etc.). *No category imposed by society need be accepted by free people.* Emancipation from whiteness leads not just to liberation for people of colour; it leads to freedom for all - even, and especially, those once imprisoned by it.

Of course, the white identity is imposed from above, and "white-skin privilege" continues to exist even for those human beings who seek to reject it. This is yet another reason for sympathy with people of colour, and solidarity with whatever political expressions they embrace. Many organisations for non-white "advancement" in the past, such as the NAACP in the United States, were led by whites. And it is this demand to lead, this arrogant knowledge of the "right way" to organise, that Black Nationalist and related expressions seek to reject. White people who presume to tell non-whites how to organise, who disparage their "racist" attempts to create spaces and communities where they can be free of white interference—these are white people who have still not rejected white privilege. The hardest thing for people used to privilege and command to accept, whatever "revolutionary" politics they claim to espouse, is that they might not be needed. Malcolm X exhorted sincere white revolutionaries to organise in their own white communities against the endemic racism that defines these communities. Here was a battle that Malcolm had no power to fight, and it was an important battle, an integral and indispensable part of the total movement. But white radicals who, uninvited, try to muscle in on organisations and movements of people of colour, operate not to liberate people of colour, but to flatter and aggrandise themselves. In the name of fighting racism, they become the worst of racists. While there are no essential racial differences between people, and "colour-blindness" might well seem a beneficial attitude to have, to be ignorant of the past and present categorisations which make these abstractions have real social consequences, or worse to deny them, is to be guilty of far worse racism than one purports to oppose.

White people are used to leading. In the history of the dominant culture, it is they who are mentioned, their politics which are celebrated. White abolitionists are given credit for fighting against slavery, their luminaries cited often in the working out of history. How often is it even mentioned, let alone emphasised, that slave revolts were happening all the time in the American South, and that these actions on the part of unheralded, anonymous people of colour for their own emancipation had as much if not more to do with the end of slavery than any actions engaged in by white abolitionists? How often is the Haitian Revolution of 1791-1803—the only successful large-scale slave uprising in human history, and after the United States,

An Ethics of Sanity

the first New World colony to overthrow European imperialism—even mentioned more than in passing, let alone given the credit for the epoch-making event that it was? Hegel, whose writings laid the foundation of Marxist and much revolutionary thought, is said by most historians to have taken his inspiration from the French Revolution of 1789; what is rarely mentioned is how much the Haitian Revolution contributed to his ideas and inspired his sense of the revolutionary progress of history. Consistently, the role of nonwhite people are ignored, written out of our consciousness, whilst the role of white people takes center stage.

It is evident that white people, being "white" people, have operated from a sense of entitlement that undermines their sincerity as revolutionaries. This entitlement is a necessary component for every status of privilege - gender, racial, class, etc. It is this entitlement that must be rejected, along with all the other aspects of privileged status. This requires an amount of humility and a willingness for deep soul-searching that is difficult to quantify. None of us are "perfect" or "pure." Knowing this, we should not hate ourselves or deny ourselves our right to humanity, our right to hate and challenge the system along with everyone else; but neither should we forget that "pride" in the sense of arrogance stems from an attitude that isolates us, that separates us from the experience of others. It is the fine line between a healthy, self-loving ego and the grandiosity of false, unhealthy egotism that we must all walk in order to be authentic. And for those of us who have privilege, this line is even finer. There is no "programme" that can be enumerated here to help you walk that line. Rather, humility and a willingness to sympathise, broadly stated, must guide you.

Liberation from the Hierarchical Delusion

A sense of entitlement is the result of privilege long unquestioned. It is a swelling of the head which eclipses the heart. It is the enticement granted by a system of hierarchy which needs a privileged caste to continue to exist, in order to frustrate solidarity with those more oppressed. This entitlement can be seen in every category of privilege, from that of gender to that of sexuality to that of race. But its most developed form, its most unapologetic and naked existence, can be found among those claiming to be an "elite." With most other privileges, fears, resentments, and other cloudier sentiments get mixed up into their conceptions. Men fear women's potential power, or resent them for their beauty, or are lashing out against them in a hatred born of their own negative self-image or unresolved pain resulting from their traumatic journey from boy to man. The white race is enlisted to hate non-whites over the fear, sometimes expressed, most often only sensed, that non-whites will rape, murder, or even enslave the whites for all the crimes of the past centuries. Homophobes fear rape as well, as well as the molestation of children - and many times, both men and women dimly remember being raped or molested at the hands of adults when they themselves were children.

But with pure elitism, there are no "resentments" going on, no sense of persecution, real or imagined, informing the prejudice. More than any other kind of privilege involving human/human relations, elitism is based on the pure, unapologetic assertion of privilege itself - with no other complications. The joy of power, the wallowing in inequality, and the basic lie that the upper class is "better" than the rest, is the core of the privilege and the prejudice. It informs every other prejudice, fuelling every other oppression, for it is the very essence of prejudice itself, prejudice for prejudice's own sake. As the most indispensable part of the structure of civilisation, through all its political and economic forms throughout history, the delusional mindset underlying elitism is the root cause of all the others.

The underlying delusion of the elite is that there needs to be one. There are "better" people, and there are "worse." The better are those who are "blessed by the gods" (as in feudal and ancient societies), or who are "intelligent and innovative" (as is assumed of the capitalist elites), or even who are "selflessly working toward a classless society" (the obnoxious refrain of the Communists). Confucius, that early justifier of civilisation and authority, spoke of the "worthy" men, opposing them to the "foolish"—in part a hopeful exhortation to the elite to act in ways "worthy" of their "worth" - their status. There is always a sense of "refinement" and "culture" with the elite, some sense of familiarity and conformity to an etiquette defined by the elite themselves to exclude the majority from it and convey a sense of belonging within it. This belonging compels the members of the elite to act "civilised" (i.e. rational, controlled, sensitive to "beauty," interested in "progress" and charitable philanthropy, etc.), to act as "gentle" men and women, even as their business and military interests tie them to the most naked and brutal acts of exploitation and extermination of whole populations around the planet. The architecture of civilisation has always attempted to create distance between the palaces of the powerful and the sites of the "dirty-work" of their civilisation, extending from the time of walls and motes to today's gated communities and suburbs to the increasingly militarised borders of the hemispheres. The "real" must never be allowed to intrude upon the blissful cocktail party of the exploiters; otherwise, the rulers might lose the will to rule.

Inhumanity on this level is simply too naked to risk viewing its nakedness, and thus a shield built of oceans and police forces and self-deceptions fuelled by universities and art galleries and restaurants and religions must hide the evil from those who profit from it. The delusion of separateness fuelling every other category of privilege must in the case of the elite come to its full potential of psychic deterioration.

How is this accomplished? By rarefying to the greatest extent possible the initial distinction between human and nonhuman that spawned the hierarchy of civilisation in the first place. The basic lie of civilisation - that we as a species need to "better ourselves" from our aboriginal, animal brutishness - has survived in tact from the time of the first civilised creation myths through the idealistic philosophies of Plato and the patriarchal ethics of Confucius to today's "scientific" assumptions and human-centred interpretations of evolutionary theory. Man is "better" the further he is from the dirt. The best men, then, are those who never get dirty. The most civilised must be those least soiled by contact with things of the earth, with "earthiness." The sign of the "worthy" man is his cultivation of artifice, from the manner in which he eats his food to the way in which he speaks his language to the aesthetics with which he learns and enjoys his culture. These signs of initiation into the folkways of the elite constitute a culture within a culture, and it is the acculturation into it that creates the greatest dependence upon the civilisation of any class or group within it - even as it grants the initiated a psychology of entitlement supposedly geared toward their independence and power.

The civilisation has always relied upon rituals, texts, and beliefs on all its levels; those at the top display these to a greater degree than any below them, with those below encouraged to imitate their "betters" as part of their allegiance to the civilisation as a whole. A "pecking order" is thus fostered amongst the classes, with each middling layer compensated for their inferiority to those above by the sop of looking down on those below. Elitism is not confined simply to the uppermost ruling class, but can be found throughout the hierarchy. White racism can be found among otherwise egalitarian-minded working class people, those for whom the implication of looking down on others would constitute the worst insult.

Such racism amongst the poorer classes often has to do with stereotypical views of non-whites as failing to perform as "good workers," as whites of the labouring classes without a clear consciousness of their exploited situation, the basic slavery of their "work ethic," often take pride. (Incidentally, such warped "class pride" also informs ableism, anti-mad prejudice, and ageism, where workers look down on the "lazy" and "unfit" as not "pulling their own weight.") In many cases, "union-labour" is simply a codeword for "skilled" labour; in the absence of an anti-systemic consciousness or memory, those workers lucky enough to be included in a union look down on the "scabs" who cannot afford dues and membership fees, leading to what Lenin called an "aristocracy of labour" devoid of solidarity and thoroughly accommodated to the system.

Many of even the richest in capitalist societies, particularly in the United States, consider themselves "middle class." But in that middle-classness is the distance from the "white trash" from whom they, by their aesthetic tastes or their education or even their "progressive" politics, distinguish themselves. Different professions are accorded status in society which may seem to do with their apparent usefulness to humanity. And yet doctors, who are arguably engaged in such meaningful work, are far more respected than teachers, without whom they would never have learned to be doctors. And neither are as essential to society as farmers and janitors, who are accorded no "professional" prestige whatsoever. "Citizenship" becomes a means of collective elitism, perhaps the most detrimental and schismatic of all human/human relations in the present moment of world civilisation. Through the elitism of First World citizenship, people of all classes, genders, and races are able to distance themselves from their fellow human beings, blinded to the sheer dumb luck of their birth on the northern side of the planet, identifying in pride and contempt with the civilisation's status quo.

To attack the root of the elitist delusion is to confront the most basic lie of all: that any self, in order to be a self, must regard itself superior to others for a sense of self-worth. From my own madness, I can speak of this dynamic of ego-formation, its authentic and inauthentic dimensions, most clearly. My voices have for the last thirteen years been desperately attempting to make me assert myself. The reason they are *so* evil to me is that they wish me to hate them - utterly, contemptuously, and without pity. Until a few weeks before I wrote these words, I was stuck. To hate them felt wrong, because I couldn't bring myself to hate the people they were (recall, they have names and personalities, and at times one or more have even been "on my side" in the fight against the rest). Yet, to fail to hate them is to lose the game, to be "weak" and cowardly, and ultimately to consent to their evil. But just a few weeks ago, I had an insight: I *did* have an ego, I *was* asserting it - precisely by believing in the path I'd been following without giving myself credit for the last thirteen years. Suddenly, I no longer had to feel weak and cowardly, or caught in unworthiness or inadequacy, for refusing such things as the value of my essential facticity (my race, my gender, my education, etc. - signs of power which they attack and want me to defend - selfishly, contemptuously, as they selfishly defend

An Ethics of Sanity

theirs). Instead, I could feel that my passion to refuse these privileges was the *essence* of my power. Since then, I've been freer of them than I've been for years.

When I first conceived this essay, I planned to talk of the Song of the "I" and contrast it with the Song of the "We," drawing this binary and siding with the latter as the soul of these ethics. But, aside from this binary being an abstraction of my experience rather than the experience itself, I've come to realise that the individual and the collective are *not* opposites. It is not necessary to subsume the ego to be a good anarchist, a good radical, or a good person. Rather, the ego and the other are themselves only separated by artificial, abstracted theory. Reality lies not in their opposition to one another, but rather in their mutual interrelation in which one grows from the other and vice versa. No healthy individual can exist outside of community, and no healthy community can exist without just about every individual in that community realising, developing, and fostering his or her own and all others' growth toward whole, healed selves. I could not write these words without believing in myself. And I could not write these words without the hope that some in the community would read and interact with them. As I write these words, I explore myself, resolve my schizophrenic splits, and develop the ego which I have all my life - and especially in the last thirteen years - been afraid to express. Every person in my community, beginning with my loved ones, but extending eventually to all who wish to read this, known or unknown to me, whether they agree, disagree, remain indifferent, add or detract, will shape these ethics into something which no longer "belong" to me, but instead to everyone.

The role of the observer, the "abstract" thinker, is the coveted role of any human hierarchy. Some of the first large-scale slavery in history was used to build one of the first monuments—the ziggurat, a staircase into the sky from which the privileged could "look down" on the rest. Atop that lofty perch, the ruler could *observe* all his land below him, in a way no earthly ruler had ever been able to do before. I am not unaware that I risk the most ludicrous irony by saying to you that I wish people could abandon abstraction and observation by giving you pages of abstraction and observation to read.

If I were to write these words in the hope of gaining adulation for using abstraction, then I would be writing these words in vain. But as many of my initial insights are shared by other people, or derived from them, and every word I use here I've learned from someone else, I am aware that literally thousands of other souls are mixed up in all this, and practically all of them are people whose names and faces I can no longer recall. Just so, as you read these words, my hope is that they will connect with ideas and experiences you already have, and those of the people you've known, and eventually you will forget the words written here, forget my name, my face, anything to do with me personally. My greatest hope is that my ethics of sanity will find a small part in your own ethics of sanity, just as the ethics of others - learned from books I've read, people I've met, even the hallucinatory voices I've had to deal with - have informed mine.

Someday, I will die and turn to dust, as will the pages on which all this is written, as the language in which it is written will be forgotten or turn into something else - if our species, or any species, manages to survive at all. And with me shall die these voices who even now mumble taunts and challenges from beyond the kitchen window beside me. No identity exists for more than an instant before becoming mixed up into all those that follow. To preserve it beyond its use, to inflict it upon the memory of future generations for its own sake - as the Pharaohs attempted to do with their slavery-built tombs - is the original source of the desire for power. To

An Ethics of Sanity

dissolve oneself into the compost that will grow future gardens is the closest to "immortality" any of us need. Anything else is delusion, born of an egotism which stems from an insecure and unhealthy self-hood.

The self-hood of the voices is based in this ugly desire. I once asked them what they considered beautiful, as if to tease out their humanity even as they tortured me. They grimly replied: PERMANENCE. This was the sole beauty they acknowledged in the world. They were not interested in opera or art for its inherent beauty, but rather for the fact that it had "stood the test of time." This is the yardstick which the most conservative appreciators of art and culture constantly apply. They hate and oppose the avant-garde, until the generations pass and it can be recuperated as "safe" for them to appreciate. The voices admire the music of Mozart. But they would be among the first to condemn him in life as a mere commoner who got above himself, a drunk and a madman. They would have easily let him die, along with all the rest of the aristocracy of his time. Mozart's beauty now lies in his permanence - and in that alone. It is a dead thing, this permanence, by its very definition. This is the ugly, oppressive, institutional reality that the highest in society have always sought to impress upon history; this is the very reason why "history" as a concept came to be invented.

As Orwell wrote: Who controls the present controls the past; who controls the past controls the future. This is the political dimension, the "how" of the perpetuation of civilisation and hierarchy. But the "why" of power and domination cannot be explained merely by observing its outward signs or the mere fact of its existence. To understand why a person, a group, a class, a race, a gender, or a species would want to assert power over another, one must confront evil in its most basic reality (as my subconscious has forced me to confront it, on an intellectual, emotional, even sensate level). This evil is selfishness; and selfishness comes from a self which forgoes the journey to true actualisation, and instead opts for a false, immature, unkind inflation and infliction of itself on all the rest. The ego, the self, the soul (whatever you call it) desires blending with others when it is most healthily developed. The draw towards conversation, the shared distractions of hobbies or sport or the partaking of food or drink with companions, the drowning of the ego in the art and music and stories of others, making love – these are ways we escape the isolation few of us relish and none can long endure. For the ego cannot exist unto itself, but must realise the palpable connection to the community of life on which it depends. The ego is only "egotistical" when it is unsure of itself, fears its unimportance, and therefore desperately compensates by seeking to assert its importance at the expense of others. The well-known dynamic of low self-esteem being the source of arrogance is true. Poverty in the self leads to miserliness of affection, lack of trust, and the illusion (and delusion) of separation.

      This was the dilemma I could not find a way to authentically resolve in my fight with the voices: how to assert myself without contempt, how to condemn them without stooping to their level and becoming cruel and hateful. But a few weeks ago, I came to the conclusion I stated above. As I was trying to wrestle with it for so many years in the battle with my voices I realised that the ego is a natural result of loving interaction with others. It is not, as the voices tried to convince me, the contemptuous, raping, hating selfishness the "game" I'm forced to play with them supposedly requires. Through the crucible of my madness, I am coming finally to health. Taking pills, going to therapy, etc., to stop the voices from speaking to me could never give me true wholeness, because the voices - as antithetical as they are to me - are an integral part of me. They are part of my mind's process of healing me from the disconnection I felt from my politics and my spirituality, which can but oppose the system and the values the voices represent if I am to be authentically "me."

I cannot ignore my own mind. Even the most horrible, nightmarish moments of my life have had a purpose—*to heal me.* This is the biggest error in the method of healing practised by modern psychiatry. A bio-medical understanding, like the older psychoanalytical method before it, assumes there's something "wrong" with the mad, that madness is a disorder to be "corrected." But painful or not, madness is no different from any other way to cope with life in this society—of finding meaning in apparent meaninglessness—a battle which all people fight. Society cannot be evaded. Even in methods of escape, still there is something one is escaping from, its shadow there despite any sunny horizon. My years of abandoning activism, an activism which I've returned to with new vigour, new love, was the reason my mind decided to "play a trick" on me, and give me hallucinations. Realising this, finally, I can begin to be free of the pain. And meanwhile, all the insights I've gained remain real to me, helping my continuing growth.

The delusion of elitism, be it expressed in communism, capitalism, or any other kind of gangsterism, stems more directly than any other form of privileged delusion from what has been called a "Napoleon complex." Because people's maturity is stunted, because they are offered the thinnest and shallowest comforts in lieu of love, they tend not really to know themselves, let alone like what they do know. They hide from others what they think of as their essential ugliness, fail to trust others, fail to trust themselves. The majority of people who feel this way sink into self-contempt, deny themselves their right to pleasure, question their worthiness to be angry at the system which has caused all this misery, and eventually learn to obey. The few others, motivated by no less a level of self-contempt, conclude that all life is based on contempt, that all is hate, and that rape is not only inevitable, but a positive *good*. Faced with the rape at the apparent core of existence, they choose to be rapists. The former was me; the latter, my voices.

But the basic lie is easily thwarted. Beauty is not the province of "refinement" or "higher culture." Beauty is every person's basic reality, and discovering it is the fundamental journey we all have the opportunity to take in life. No one is ugly, except those who *choose* to be ugly. If everyone were as ugly as Hobbes' *Leviathan* would have it, our species would have died out long ago. The fact that we have survived, even through the long eras of exploitation and misery that is civilisation, and have even managed some measure of generosity and idealism in its shadow, is testament to the basic tendency of people at the least to strive towards indifference, if not actually goodness, in their dealings with one another.

Of course, the world right now is ugly. And people caught up in the delusions of ugliness, who embrace cynicism, who deny the possibility of meaning, are all of us at times. Elitism as I've come to have known it, as expressed by my subconscious mind in direct intercourse with my consciousness, could not be possible without the basic myth of unworthiness, the lack of love for oneself, and the resulting shrinking from the risk of loving others. No privilege is possible without this disconnection, no oppression possible without the cynical contempt for the worth of others. The antidote to elitist delusions, as all such delusions, is realising on the animal level, the sensate and emotional level, the proximity of oneself to other people, and to the whole community of life which remains alive despite millennia of abuse. Distance can only be mitigated by abandoning it in favour of connection, a process greatly rewarding personally, and essential to our collective survival as a planet.

Again, these are not sentimental or mystical assertions, any more than any assertion is tinged with sentiment and mysticism. It can be demonstrated by following out any line of logic you choose. The basic molecular reality of space is fuzziness, its lack of clear boundaries between objects. On all larger levels, the same truth holds. Male and female, black and white, night and day—these binaries always have their twilight spaces, their in-between-ness, which renders any abstract system but an approximation of a reality which is vast and ineffable. The human species is not separate from other species, as it is becoming clearer and clearer by the day. To proceed from the assumption that the human animal is "better" is the same as proceeding from the idea that it is "worse." *Ranking itself is the problem.*

Testing and evaluating the "worth" of things is a preoccupation of madness, as my own over-determined reality (which at times of crisis involves every single object I see jumping out at me and demanding my immediate evaluation) tends to see hidden meaning in everything. The ego in crisis clings to scales of value by which it constantly measures everything. The only difference between the mad and the "sane" in this regard is that for the latter, these scales of value are supported by the consensus of society. My ego was forced to form in conflict with voices of power, and for the past thirteen years I've never felt certain about my worth or worthiness. Love of others I had; indeed it was often all I had. But love of myself had to be developed, gradually, painfully, before my mind could begin to become whole once again. And now, as a queer who goes through the process of intense reflection of "coming out," I consider myself *healthier* for my years of madness than I ever was before it.

The ego must have the love of others to become itself. And in order to receive the love of others, the ego must be generative of love. Community is the catalyst by which the ego becomes itself. Liberated communities, or communities of resistance, must be understood as societies of free and loving individuals, living in common. Any form of privilege, unquestioned and unchallenged, poisons the community, divides it. Egalitarianism, sharing resources, deciding in common - these are the prerequisites of social health, as well as the personal health of all the individuals within that society. Civilisation, while pretending to unite people, in fact sows the seeds of discord, creating and sustaining conflicts, and perpetuating disharmony. The project of hierarchy requires inadequacy, institutionalised immaturity, fear of oneself and others. The antidote to this is anarchy, whether those living in such a state call themselves "anarchists" or not. Beauty, like sexual liberation, like "lifestyle" choices in tandem with "serious" politics, like the humility and honesty with which one looks at oneself, like love of the natural world and the people who are - even after ten thousand years of living in delusion and denial - still but a part of it; these are not things "on the side" of liberation. They are quintessential aspects of the total picture. No authority, no hierarchy, no privilege can be tolerated in oneself. For all are delusions of distance, and thus the paths to madness.

Sanity, as we have defined the term over these pages, can be seen as *wholeness*. My own sanity was compromised by living in a society of disconnection and division, struggling to survive in the midst of economic hardship, political uncertainty, and biological and spiritual vulnerability to the negative aspects of madness. From traumas in my early childhood family dynamic, molestation by peers at the onset of puberty,

An Ethics of Sanity

class oppression and ostracism during formative school years, abuse suffered in relationships with friends and lovers, betrayals by close comrades and the loss of my whole world view - and from growing up with the modalities of maleness, whiteness, and First World citizenship - I suffered schisms between my mind and body, my reason and my emotions. It was this schizophrenia which my schizophrenic delusions and hallucinations sought to cure. I have been made whole over time, though I know my journey to individuation will never be truly over until I die. These ethics inform my ego in its healthy, newly formed reality. The very process of writing them has helped me understand and appreciate it. And I know, as part of my chosen identity, that the identities of many others blend with mine as the process is completed.

      Over the course of my battle with the voices, I've learned one more crucial insight, one which lends itself to ending this exploration of an ethics of sanity in an insane world. And it is this insight that both helps me find my own personal freedom from the negative effects of madness, and one that I offer to guide you in choosing your own path to recovery, for yourself and for your world. With this insight, which has to do with the nature of abstraction, myth, and madness, I'd like to conclude this essay.

Chapter V: The Many Paths to Sanity

I, like many people, have changed my mind about things like politics, spirituality, and how I view my place in the world many times over the course of my lifetime. For much of my life, these changes have been accompanied by crisis, even trauma, as I've gone through the painful process of losing one world view to gain another. But never were the crises of these changes more acute than during the half-year of my initial manifestation of full-blown schizophrenia, the time when my voices first appeared to me as they are. During those six months between April and September 1997, I was forced to radically rethink the politics and spirituality that I'd taken for granted during the preceding years. The catalyst for this rethinking, which led eventually to the ethics embodied in these pages, was and remains my madness, and particularly the desperate need to fight a battle with personalities opposed to me for reasons intimately connected to my radicalism.

At the time, I'd been drifting politically, having lost a comfortable world view (Trotskyist-Marxism) which had answered all my questions and allowed me a way to live in opposition to the world, all with the consoling solidarity of comrades. But my comrades came to betray me, and my world view had consequently proved untenable. I'd become interested in Communism around the time of the First Gulf War in 1991, and from that time to the turn of the year 1993-94, I'd been involved in building a fledgling organization with the Trotskyites I'd met during the war. But in early 1994, a variety of things led me to break with the organisation (which soon thereafter dissolved), and with the loss of both comrades and a comradely world view, I began to become disillusioned with activism. By the end of 1994,

An Ethics of Sanity

I had drifted from activism almost entirely, taking up instead the course of fiction writing as a calling. I spent the next two years trying to find a way to live, work, and still have time to write. I regularly went without meals, drank a lot, and spent a significant amount of this time nearly homeless. These "starving artist" economic privations undoubtedly helped speed along my deterioration. But the illusion I pursued - the idea that I could live without politics of resistance and accommodate myself somehow to life in a bourgeois society - was the real reason for the onset of my madness.

Without Communism, I found it hard to justify revolution in my mind; and yet, my heart still revolted at the thought of living without radicalism. It was this schizophrenic split between the cynicism and hopelessness of my mind and the desperation for a better world still burning in my heart that led to a crisis of ego - for I could not believe in myself to fight for revolution, could not justify it to others or even reason it out to myself - yet I could not give up the dream. Once sharp in debate and confident, I found myself lagging, fearing confrontation, eventually becoming shy and turning inward. I passed up many opportunities to voice opposition to ugly things around me; yet I could not forget they were ugly. This lack of ego is something which came to be resolved through the trial of my madness, a process still going on even as I write these words. I was forced to confront all the ugliness I sensed in the form of self-accusation, making myself fight a battle within because I had failed to fight it outside.

In the course of dealing with the initial paranoia of being pursued by someone or something, and then the further descent into the Hell of "hearing" and at times "seeing" my pursuers in the flesh, I was challenged to maintain my heartfelt but confused ideals in the face of a grim reality. My first identity in this process was my identity as an "artist." I fought the forces and pressures of my society to "get a job," to "settle down," to "grow up," and all the rest of acquiescence to life in this society, in order to pursue my writing. This rebellious, yet essentially isolating and apolitical pursuit, was assailed from all directions. I was made to feel doubt about my ability to get published, and even the worthiness of my work to merit publication. While these doubts are shared by virtually every writer, every artist, the way my mind works made the threat of losing my "lifestyle" for the misery of submitting to capitalism very frightening. How my family, particularly my father, treated me on this score was among the first manifestations of this threat.

As I continued to spiral down, I began to mishear and misinterpret comments by others, and then I began to think songs on the radio, programmes and commercials on TV, and headlines in newspapers were all voicing this threat, taunting me, mocking me, daring me to continue to write even as the worth of the project was denigrated from all sides. As I came finally to hear voices, the initial conflict between us centred round questions of what an "artist" was, what "selling out" entailed, and whether my pursuit of art was "laziness," "shirking responsibility," "arrogance," or even indulging in "bourgeois decadence" and aspiring to bourgeois privilege. I fought hard for my vision, but I eventually came to realise that being an apolitical artist was not authentic enough for me. I needed to find a modus for action involving some greater solidarity, some understanding of my place in the world beyond my own individual, isolated reality.

The next phase of identity I embraced was a radical "American" understanding, a "radical patriotism" inspired by the Constitutional Militia movement of the mid-1990s. My sympathies for the simple, homegrown radicalism of these misunderstood, maligned poor

An Ethics of Sanity

farming folk, who inspired me to begin writing my second novel, helped me oppose the classism and liberal hypocrisy that reigned under the Clinton administration.

It allowed me a way of embracing a tradition from which all my Democrat/labour/urban/liberal background and later anti-American Communism had distanced me. I got to know Republicans, conservatives, even fundamentalist Christians, on a level of sympathy I'd previously thought impossible. Yet my radical Americanism could also embrace the whole tradition of the American Left, and as much as any libertarian, militia conception, I took inspiration from such cultural icons as Woody Guthrie and the Weavers, who often commingled their radical, even Communist sentiments with a patriotic regard for the working people and poor of America. All of it together was a vision of America that has and continues to inspire many ordinary people - not only to fight the government's wars, but also to fight against them. Armed with this certainty, I set myself in opposition to the mainstream of the dominant parties, corporate *and* government bureaucracy (represented quite neatly by the Republican and Democratic Parties, respectively), the police state which killed the activists in the MOVE organisation in the 1980s and slaughtered the still largely unmourned Branch Davidians at Waco, Texas in the 1990s. I utilised patriotic conceptions of a mythic, liberatory American "spirit" to oppose the machinations of a sell-out, fascist (or, if you like, communist) American government.

For a time, this paradigm served me against the voices, who could not challenge my revolutionism. Even as they claimed their capitalist hierarchy as the soul of America, they were forced to consider my anarchic interpretation of America as possibly invalidating their own claims of patriotism. Rather than reject America, burn the flag, etc., I took up the cause of America more radically, more *deeply,* than my adversaries. I was *more* patriotic, *more* American than their champagne-lunch-in-Paris classist privilege, calling them not simply ugly, but framing their ugliness in terms of their being traitors to the very ideology which justified them. Connection to my "mother country" - whose ideals I felt went against not only fascism and communism, but aristocracy in all its forms - helped me for a time against the voices, confusing them, consternating them.

But eventually, they prevailed in their logic, pointing out the basic untenability (for me) of a patriotic - even a "revolutionary" patriotic - perspective. I was told, convincingly, that most Americans did not see their country the way I did, and that the only "comrades" I might have had were rural white Christians who most probably would have hated me for being queer, irreligious, counter-cultural, formerly leftist, etc. As no one in my immediate circle espoused my beliefs, I felt this isolation even more acutely. And thus, against the voices and without comrades, I found myself turning in desperation to a Deity, to whom I'd not turned since finding Communism (and thus atheism) years before. Of course, my God (or, Goddess) was no god of complacency, that grim opiate paralysing so many in the working class. No, my God was an *Allah*, a *God of Revolution.* As my voices were atheists, scorning religiosity as weak-willed sops for the masses, demanding like a Communist elite that I look straight into the face of their power with no mystical escape or divine recourse, this idea, as my previous patriotism, was a living insult to them. And, as my radical patriotism had been before it, my radical religion continued the process of reducing not just them personally, but their whole "game" - their very honour as members of a hierarchy - to a humiliating lie.

So, beginning with an amused contempt for me

An Ethics of Sanity

as a pseudo-artist, to an increasing annoyance with me as a better "patriot" than they were, my stinging critique of their "ungodly" privilege and power began to really infuriate them. They sought to prove to me that I was alone, making it even more their mission to destroy me than it had been before. But I *believed* in my God. And I *knew* that revolution would come, even if I'd never live to see it, even if they were destined to remain in power well after I was dead. *They would fall.* This unshakable certainty provided me with a means to go on. My heart was fully supported by a power outside myself, brought to me by the benevolent spirits of Jim Morrison, Virginia Woolf, and Malcolm X, who spoke to me as angels. But my mind, my need for logic, continued to press on me. And it was thus that I in renewed desperation returned to the reading of my Marx and my Lenin, and became for a few weeks a Trotskyite once again.

They mocked me for this, too, but within a few days, they were dumbfounded by the greater certainty of my logic. I began to reach out to some friends, including my feminist lover, to build some kind of "organisation" of revolutionaries. In order to prepare ourselves for our activism, my comrades read (and I reread) pamphlets which took apart the hard, economic reality of capitalism, exposing its contradictions, and we laughed at the inability of the voices to prevail. I recall one time explaining the labour theory of value to my close friend, and having the voices taunt me beyond my window. I smiled to them and taunted back, haughtily, "*disprove it, then.*" They pulled away in utter defeat and rasped: *WE HATE YOU.*

After that, they began to really want me dead. I had exposed them as purveyors of bad art, then traitors to the real spirit of America, then denied them even the opiate of their own morality. Now I said to them, simply, effortlessly: your system is worse than simply banal, unAmerican, or evil; your system *simply does not work* -

and there is *nothing* you capitalists can do about it! Now they could not assail my heart *or* my mind. So again, they concentrated on my worthiness, my right to hold such a thought and feeling in the first place. Did I not see, they taunted, that your friends will abandon you? And had I not *myself* betrayed them? I was paranoid of my friends, after all, paranoid too of my father. Was I not the worst of sell-outs, actually, despite all my pretty words and my delusions of grandeur?

These were the paradigms I found to bolster my sense of revolution; these are but a few of the many that people have used and continue to use to understand and act against a society of oppression which takes so many forms. Of course, I continued to develop from here, after medications and counselling and hard-won insights made the voices retreat a little into my subconscious, only to flare up from time to time - most recently shortly after the death of my father in late 2006. Even in the last few months, my concepts of "anarchy" have gone from red to green to pink and back again, from anarcha-feminism to syndicalism to toying with primitivism to this essay (in which elements of these, and many other things, have merged with Mad activism and a Mad perspective—still a quite new locus of oppression in the minds of even anarchists, let alone mainstream society, at the time I write these words). I now live in a collective house with a group of comrades and friends, along with my primary lover, who shares with me a Mad perspective - and so much more.

The initial insight of distance and the need for wholeness which has informed everything in this essay has been actualised in living in community with these good folks, and the presence of even those here whom I do not know very well yet has in the last weeks helped me heal from flare-ups of my schizophrenic hallucinations and paranoia. And it is this process which has brought home to me the essential falsity of the

An Ethics of Sanity

dichotomy between "individualism" and "collectivism" that has divided anarchists into competing schools of thought since as far back as the nineteenth century, but which I maintain is an entirely abstract dichotomy existing only in delusion. The day-to-day of living with comrades and friends, its challenges and its rewards, more than melts this "on paper" dichotomy into one resolved, whole reality that is difficult to put into words, but whose authenticity I feel manifested around me daily.

The voices have disappeared lately, almost entirely. This proves to me the worth of love, sensual, emotional, mental, and spiritual, bringing me out of the world of dissociation and isolation into the warm reality of other people. But in addition to loving others, and receiving their love, I must begin to love myself. The ego-strength I'm forming even as I write these words is allowing me finally to answer the question I stated above that the voices put to me all those years ago: Am I "worthy" of my ideals?

Most of the above has centred around modalities of privilege. All of it has centred around distance and abstraction as the essential props and products of privilege. I cannot say, after writing all this, that I - or anyone else - is "perfect" or "pure" in regard to rejecting the delusions of privilege or the sick desire for power. I know that I, as one who lives in this society, and has imbibed thirty-seven years of its poisons, can never be completely free of the fears and inadequacies which tempt me to take from others selfishly, to think of them in ugly ways from time to time, to fail to love them as truly as I feel I should, or as truly as they deserve. Unconsciously, I surely have bolstered the system of oppression whose ugly values make themselves felt even within the interrelations of my anarchist housemates. As a male-bodied human being, I may always take for granted a certain safety, comfort, and entitlement to state my views, even to walk down the street at night, without fear of serious reprisal. As a pale-complexioned human being, I may take for granted my ability to write and to publish and to act upon radical views in ways that my comrades of colour take much greater risks in expressing, as the racist state has always and continues to police and persecute radicals of colour in ways only occasionally felt by those of my melanin-count. And as one versed with at least some of the hallowed canon of my culture's writings and ideas, and with an ability to manipulate symbols and play language games more easily than other people, I will always feel a greater sense of entitlement, and be taken more seriously, than many other of my fellow human beings who right now slave their lives away building computers such as the one I am typing all this into, poisoned with chemicals and starved on pittance-wages and threatened with prison and death when they try to revolt, or even to unionise. I have the opportunity because of my education and my First World status and my childhood familiarity with English to advance my ideas in ways so many of my brothers and sisters round the globe will never have. All this is not to mention my privilege over the animal and plant life which built and fuels my house, provides my food and clothing, and generates the electricity by which I write all this, destroying the environment and driving so many species daily to extinction.

That said, I try. And that is all any of us can do. To be "ethical" is not to be "perfect." Perfection itself is a delusion, an idealism, an abstraction, which has gone hand in hand with all the deterioration and derangement of the history of civilisation. The delusion of a "perfect" world, from Plato's "ideal plane" to Marx's "end of history," is nothing but the "refinement" of the upper classes, the "purity" of the white race, the "rationality" of the Victorian, scientific male, the "mental health" of the conformist, and the "correctness" of any radical political platform. It is nonsense. Utter, unadulterated magical thinking. Its pursuit condemns one to sadness at the very least. More probably, it leads to cynicism, complacency, and contempt. The myth of something "perfect" or "pure" leads to dissatisfaction with what is natural, earthy, and real. Disgust with oneself, an inability to connect with others, and the denial of pleasure and ecstasy - these inevitably follow.

What my experience with shifting paradigms of revolution proves to me, along with the insights I've gained from Zen Buddhism, Postmodern philosophy, Chaos Theory, and various poetries and works of art, is that no "one truth" about anything can be attained in words, no truth-claims can be made absolutely with any one way of looking at something. Reality is ineffable, beyond us. The best we can do is try to find some clunky, imperfect mechanism to help capture its beauty, always remembering it is not these abstractions, these clunky tools, which are beautiful, but that thing beyond them which we can try to sense, and with the common reference points of the shared abstractions, try to sense with others. This is the value of myth, of paradigm. If it helps us to get together in a community which gives us the love we need to fight the hate - then it is a good myth. If it fails in this regard, even anarchy (my chosen paradigm of resistance) serves only to divide us, encourage our distrust and disconnection from other radicals and from the human race in general, and makes us feel superior because of our "insight" and "intelligence" and "forward-thinking." What are we, then, but yet another lousy elite, privileged and contemptuous and mean?

Anarchists should not make the age-old mistake of believing their analysis or their theory is any more "truth in itself" than any other clunky tool of abstraction. It is not in the abstraction that the human race will emancipate themselves from hierarchy, but in the revolutionary actions they will take to make themselves free. The project of revolution, the urge to revolt, is at least as old as history. As long as there have been modalities of hierarchy, as long as there have been people categorised to rule and others categorised to be dominated, there have been elements of the latter who have resisted. At times, their revolts have made the history-books and even remain in popular consciousness today, like Spartacus' failed slave revolution, or the successful slave revolution in Haiti at the turn of the 19th Century. Other times, history records them, but they're not widely known, buried by historians and the legions of the media, so one must dig: like the first city-wide general strike in Europe—long before there were Marxist "Internationals" and analyses—the Revolt of the Ciompi (unorganized textile-workers) in 1378 Florence; or the very first recorded strike action of a wage-working proletariat, that of tomb-builders and tomb-painters in an Egyptian village four thousand years ago.

    Many, many more movements have been lost to history and human memory; but I, for one, believe they must have positively abounded. Many of what we know as traditional, even authoritarian institutions – governments, religions – are but the ruins of once-revolutionary movements, now long recuperated by the society of hierarchy and turned into their opposite. Movements we've been taught to think of as "cultural," "artistic," "religious," "philosophical," even "scientific" - as opposed to the strictly "political" - arose from the urge to revolt against hierarchy, and went hand-in-hand with the political and social movements for radical change. Our histories have been taught to us in a way to obscure the popularity of radicalism in the cultures of our ancestors. As much as I may speak with love for the concept of Revolution, as a political but also a

An Ethics of Sanity

spiritual calling, it is really just a commonplace and natural reaction which eventually comes to most everyone who endures oppression. As I accepted my Queerness when I was nineteen, and I am coming to accept my Madness now, finally, for its good as well as its pain, most everyone must come to decolonize their minds and hearts from the forces trying to define and thus destroy them, if they are finally to make the choice to live.

I have no reason to believe this process has not been going on since the beginning of human hierarchy. Hierarchy dehumanizes, renders its victims "animals," thus "things," thus eventually dead. The assertion of independence from such an inhuman system is the only way to truly *be* a human being; and as a human being is an animal and a part of the world's existence, the urge to revolt against injustice is the most natural thing, a matter of emotion, of instinct, as much as theory or "higher" thought. A human necessity, it must have always been a constant of human history, and so it shall remain. The underlying spirit of revolution combines reason with love and hate, the material and the mystical, and it has been felt by slaves ever since the first thug master impressed them into building his ziggurat. If the slaves had had to wait for the development of the paradigm we now call anarchism, with its modern socio-economic and largely secular critique, there would have been no revolutions before some time in the early nineteenth century. That people *did* rise up against their oppressors long before then shows they can do so with paradigms other than anarchism. And it shows, too, that they still can do so even now.

One of the reasons I wrote this essay was to get to this point. Anarchism, I should say again, is my chosen paradigm, the way I rationalise my sentiments toward revolution, my hatred of hierarchy and my hope for change. I once embraced Trotskyism for precisely the same reasons. What I learned from rejecting Trotskyism, and then later from my adoption and rejection of other paradigms during my crisis, is the valuing of the diversity of myth, and the possibility of the coexistence of widely differing perceptions within any movement or community. No two anarchists agree on what constitutes anarchy (the joke I was told by a comrade when I discovered the community I now live in is that if you get five anarchists in a room, there'll be at least ten definitions of anarchism in that room). With such divergence even among advocates of anarchy, how likely is it that the entire human race would ever agree to one "platform" of "points of unity" - even if the state and capitalism were done away with, and people actually began the project of living anarchically?

The likely answer, it seems to me, is that people *can* live in anarchy, even if they don't all call it anarchy. Just as I've known religious folk, even traditional, conservative folk, who will grant the people in my community the compliment that we are living "Christian lives" - simply their word for loving lives, a kind of earthly heaven. Their "Kingdom of God" would look very much like my "state of anarchy" - or any sincere revolutionary of a Communist persuasion might term communism, a "workers' paradise." All these things have been used by various people to describe my collective house, which we have named "the Asylum" - because it is a safe-haven for us all, and is the kind of help the mental hospital is supposed to be (though we know those asylums rarely or ever were such loving places).

The enemy - the system of hierarchy, authority, the state, capitalism, and all its many oppressions - will, like everything else, be perceived through many eyes and in many ways. But what history proves, over and over again, is that when people assert their dignity and their right to freedom from tyranny, they tend to strike at the same enemy - an enemy far more ancient than the

An Ethics of Sanity

last few centuries of modern capitalism, an enemy that has its roots in the earliest ugly urge to power. And they strive to establish decolonized spaces, communities of resistance, autonomous zones, which are places where love is defended as a revolutionary value.

I would think it incumbent upon us to maximize our forces against the common enemy of many names, as much as possible. For only with the greatest number of people are we likely to actually win - to save our species, and all species, from a monstrous system which will go on ruining the planet until there is no more planet left to ruin. And given that perceptions differ, and that no paradigm is itself the truth, we should find a way to express and understand revolutionary sentiment in the most flexible terms we can. Those motivated by revolutionary sentiment have in the past and continue to gravitate toward differing loci of oppression as their site of activism, according to what affects them personally. The different emphases can coexist within a larger movement, provided connections between them are allowed. Solidarity among differing paradigms certainly can - and must - exist; the key to the solidarity lies in understanding that it is *the same system - the same enemy* - which is responsible for all these oppressions - and working together on different projects, each of us fight against a monster so big and powerful that none of our different projects will come to fruition without putting the whole monstrous thing finally to death.

Anarchism, like communism, tends to view itself as a more totalising politic than what many disparage as "identity" politics. Such things as organising around questions of colour and race, or gender and sexuality, can be seen as parochial, as "missing the big picture." Yet, these identity politics can often be the starting point for seeing the total picture, the paths to a more inclusive solidarity. As the above pages have examined, no total picture can be complete without noting the significance of all the various kinds of privilege which together make the system run. "Narrow nationalism" is a term I borrow from one of my closest comrades who, though not an anarchist but a Puerto Rican *independentista* and community activist, shares with me a radical perspective against civilisation and capitalism, and whose sensitivity to questions of sexism, homophobia, and anti-mad prejudice has been integral in the formation of my own anarchy over the years.

Narrow nationalism applies to those in a particular community who feel their own particular oppression is the only one worth talking about, and who further fail to find solidarity even with those communities similarly oppressed. This is of course a danger with an identity-politic perspective, a key reason why so many radicals reject identity politics outright. But the reverse of identity politics - attempting a totalising analysis which downplays the privileges of socially engineered identities as "on the side" or even a "distraction" from a serious political perspective - is similarly doomed to failure. Clearly, anarchism must become even *bigger* than it is now, and in that development, identity politics can and should inform anarchism's big picture.

The creation of revolutionary narratives and radical paradigms many times has to do with a reckoning of the significance of identities. This should surprise no one. Identity is the first site of oppression a person deals with. Those who can afford the luxury of not dealing with identity are almost always those whose identities are connected with privilege. It is relatively easy for a middle or upper class heterosexual Caucasian male to ignore the "identity question," because his culture does not denigrate him for being who he is. It is a very different story for a person forced to deal with being devalued on the basis of her mandated social status, who must react against the categorisation, think about it, and reconfigure what it means if she is to assert her humanity. Even so, it is virtually impossible for her to completely escape it. Thus, it is the height of arrogance and ignorance for a person of privilege to tell one disadvantaged that she should simply "ignore" her identity, when she *must* deal with it every day of her life, as well as all the oppressions which it causes her to experience.

Those identity-politics which are revolutionary are those which configure identity according to an anti-systemic perspective. Those which are reactionary - "narrow nationalist" - are those which accept and affirm these socially-constructed identities uncritically as they are. At times, the same myths can lead to *either* perspective. Feminism which does not challenge the roots of masculine domination, which encourages women to ascend to positions of power within a sexist society rather than criticise the society as *itself* the source of the sexism - this "feminism" is reactionary, counter-revolutionary. Some might say that it isn't even really feminism at all. Politics of national or racial liberation, such as Black Nationalism or Pan-Africanism or the struggles of indigenous peoples for sovereignty or the many battles against colonialism and neocolonialism around the world, which fail to critique the economic structure of white supremacy in the world advance no one of colour. The few tokens who do rise to positions of power within the white supremacist, capitalist society serve their white masters, and the best they can hope for is to personally "pass" for white, leaving the vast majority of people of colour far down at the bottom of the hierarchy. Queer liberationists who do not affirm choice in matters of sexuality, who do not affirm sexuality as positively good and free and understand that it is straight-ness - the privilege of the normative, the conformity to the misery of the sex-roles - which is the problem, are nothing but Gay. They condemn themselves to being a mere essentialist, assimilationist minority within Straight society, one destined to organise, market, and subordinate themselves into at best a second-class version of Straight. Workers who organise as workers, but fail to connect their economic struggle to larger questions of human liberation, or who think of the "working class" as somehow more "stable," more "educated," more "dedicated" or more "advanced" than the poor "lumpen proletariat" or the "backward peasantry" - or who yet use their origins as a kind of aristocracy in dealings with members of other classes - are elitists, plain and simple. Communism - and even anarchism - which extols the virtues of "the workers" without seeing the other potentials for identity among them - as well as knowing that each "worker" is a person with a unique subjectivity, most of which is expressed and experienced when away from her job - is no philosophy of liberation. Class-centred analyses are no more essentially correct than any other oppression-centred world view. Economics do not exist in isolation from the rest of human experience, and while an economic awareness is important, even essential, to informing a world view of liberation, it is not in itself a guarantor of liberation.

While the above examples of narrow-nationalist "identity politics" are geared toward recuperation by the system, they are by no means the *only* identity politics. Politics focusing on masculine or straight domination, or on white supremacy, or on class hierarchy or the oppression of the state, as well as those focusing on the oppressions of ableism, ageism, educational (or intellectual) elitism, the exclusion of the many people who do not fit into the narrow beauty standard, the tyranny of "normalcy" and its marginalising of the mad, the enslavement and extermination of nonhuman organisms - all of these can lead to a wider understanding, a more totalising critique of society as a whole. Contemporary anarchy is a vast range of identity, and it cannot be spoken of without the awareness of the feminist, the queer, the non-white, the counter-cultural, the environmentalist along with the more traditional "labour" and "state" questions informing it. With other radicalisms, the same tendency can increasingly be felt. "Non-anarchist" radical feminisms have gone beyond a strictly "woman-centred" analysis to embrace class, race, sexuality, etc. And many "non-anarchist" anti-colonial struggles (revolutionary nationalist, religion-centred, even Marxist) include elements of feminism in their analysis and their organising. The trend toward a more totalising narrative implicating *the whole civilisation* as the enemy is gaining momentum in all quarters. While some "platform" of "political unity" may never come (and perhaps never should), efforts to bridge differing radicalisms into an ethos of solidarity seem more and more likely to succeed.

Religion, like identity-politics, can lead one to accept the dictates of the system, allow oneself to be co-opted by the power structure, and surrender to the ugly pecking order encouraged by it all, in which practically all of us are raped and rape in turn. Yet history proves time and time again that such potential is far from the only one possible. Revolutions against authority have been conducted successfully at different times and places using, for instance, the Christian religion (cf. the Anabaptists during the Reformation, the more recent radical efforts of Liberation Theology in Latin America and elsewhere, not to mention the earliest years of Christianity's opposition to the Roman empire). Some today even utilise the Christian religion to better express anarchy itself. Radical forms of Islam have likewise been part of liberation struggles, from the Khajarite opposition to early authoritarianism in the Islamic world shortly after Muhammad's death, to the fusing of Islam with Black Liberation in the United States in the mid-twentieth century, as typified by Malcolm X, to the unsettling yet undeniably compelling use of Islam as a contemporary means of opposing the empire of Western capitalism, particularly the United States, Israel, and their collaborationist puppets in the Middle East.

A degree of Paganism, Earth-centered and Nature-based spirituality, has informed radicals from the proto-socialist William Blake through to today's Earth Liberation Front. Buddhism, Hinduism, traditional African, American Indian, and Australian Aboriginal beliefs, syncretisms like Santeria and Voodoo and Rastafarianism - all of these have informed anti-Western struggles for national and racial liberation over the last centuries. Clearly, Marx's condemnation of religion purely as an "opiate" keeping people docile and willing to obey is one ignorant of history. Yet many anarchists (and other secular revolutionists) condemn religiosity outright as antithetical to radicalism, refuse to work with the religious, and disrespect and denigrate religiously-based movements as inherently reactionary.

The revolutionary potential of a religious paradigm, like that of any other kind of abstract system, has less to do with its logical, literal content than it does with the personal reasons - as much emotional as rational - for which an individual chooses to adopt it. People are attracted to paradigms and narratives of all sorts only partially because of their logical content. Sometimes it is the emotional meaning, or "image" of adherence to a paradigm like religion, that comprises the main reason for choosing it. "Lifestyle" choices involving even something as loosely logical as a style or a subculture can be a compelling part of the process of reckoning a revolutionary identity, and can lead one to radical action. Religious choice operates in the continuum of a "higher meaning" for one's life than that offered by secularist, utilitarian, meaningless capitalism. Surely, this higher meaning can lead one to look for a

An Ethics of Sanity

"pie in the sky," and shrink from revolution; yet, the vision of such an "eternal reward" can as easily serve to comfort the faithful engaged in acts of selflessness and bravery beyond what many who do not believe in such a reward might be able to do. This is simply historically true, the examples too numerous to name. And if it was true in the past, it can and will be again in the future.

It should not surprise anyone that people, on their own and without any "tutelage" from any "revolutionary intellectuals," will often choose to oppose the oppressive system in which they're forced to live. The sentiment towards revolt is as natural as the almost universal rebelliousness exhibited by young children, who "act up" and "misbehave" when they are forced to obey the unnatural authority of parents, babysitters, schools, and churches (to name but a few). No one has to "teach" rebellion against authority to four and five year olds. It is a natural tendency in the human animal - as in most other animals, both "wild" and "tame" - to resist the domination of another. It is this natural, primal tendency which makes me feel confident that eventually anarchy will come to be.

The difference between this primal, personal rebellion and what we call "radicalism" lies not in the essential nature of the rebellion, which is natural and emotional, as well as near-universal; the difference lies in the alignment of the logical, rational parts of the organism with this emotional desire. In other words, in order to become radical, one must connect one's personal urge to rebel with a sense of solidarity with others, similarly moved, in order to form what become communities of resistance, larger movements and coalitions. This is where the adoption of radical paradigms comes in. They appeal to the logic as well as to the emotions. Adopting them (and everyone adopts a paradigm of some kind - either for radicalism or against it — supposed "neutrality" ultimately just defending the status quo) allows a person to approach the dominant paradigm of the society in a way which integrates a logical sense of what is wrong with the dominant paradigm with the initial, emotional urge to rebel against it, and thus to strategise how to actualise the rebellion. It allows a means to link one's own ego—something suppressed by the society universally at some time or other—with other egos, similarly (or differently) suppressed. This is how movements for radical change always come about.

All the "sentimental" values I've been sharing all through this essay, the exhortations to "love" against society's hate, the need to wage a personal revolution against the tyranny of ourselves, to rid ourselves of our cultural conditioning which accepts and perpetuates privilege, are as one with the most primal, "selfish" urges toward ego-formation. The ego is assaulted by society. *Every ego is assaulted by society.* One can argue that the disadvantaged, those "other" to society in some central way, are more assaulted by society's evil voices than the privileged; yet, the ego-dystonic voices of society attack the egos of the privileged as well - indeed the egos in their cases are perhaps the most perverted and mutilated of all. For, in the case of those cajoled into identifying with the dominant castes, there is a level of self-policing mandated by the adoption and acceptance of the role, and it is this urge to police oneself that comes to seem "natural" in the individual - the very definition of the ego in that person's own inner eye.

Revolution, the radical rejection of society's longstanding system of oppression, is sanity. The only ego that has hope of truly developing to its full potential as a "snowflake" - all one is meant to be - is one who rejects the abstracted categories it is given, and finds instead its own self-defined, experiential self-hood. Integral in that process is finding others who feel and think in similar ways about the categories, and share the experience of rejecting them. Support, especially support given early on, can better equip one to stand against the evils of this civilisation, and become oneself. And support received encourages support extended; this is the nullification of the false dichotomy between "individual" and "collective," the very soul of true community. This is love.

Everything in our society seems geared increasingly to isolating us, to distancing us from one another. And, as these pages have argued, civilisation could not continue in its present form without the perpetuation of this distancing, without the engineering of privileged castes to keep up the cycle of rape and being raped in turn that is the dance of this culture. Love goes against this hate, this selfishness, this fear and isolation. This love is essential to my sanity, both internally and externally. It is not simply a choice; it is my very survival. And ethics based in love, both of the self and the community, inevitably leads one to fight for love's survival against a world of insanity. However we conceive the particulars, the solution unites us. We are one with the Earth, all species, all people. Let us fight for that wholeness, that sanity, in every way our snowflakes lead us.

In Closing

Identity politics have been the main thrust of much of post-60s radicalism, supplanting more "grand narrative" style politics such as anarchism, or more notably, the many schools of Marxist thought which once enjoyed such a central status in theorising liberation. This development is well known, almost cliché, and as much as many have lauded it, many more have lamented it for "losing the focus" we supposedly had before with more totalising politics. Grappling with this development was a primary reason for my writing this essay.

I hope with the above words to show the essential lack of contradiction between the two approaches (i.e. the "big picture" and the "specific identity"), as all politics of real liberation must concern itself with all the many specific oppressions inherent in civilised society, as well as provide the impetus for solidarity among the many oppressed groups, realising through consideration of all these different oppressions the common root of all of them—delusions of privilege, fuelled by and in turn sustaining the distance at the base of civilisation's psychology.

Just as the grand narratives often failed to account for the profusion and complexity of oppressions, so there is certainly the danger that a "narrow nationalist" interpretation of a given identity politic will similarly fail to help us in dismantling this monstrous machine which manufactures all our oppressions as a matter of course. People are not often given the nurturing love necessary for developing a truly positive self-image. Given this, most of us compensate for our essential self-hatred by revelling in our own victimisation, both because it justifies our failures in generating love for others and, more authentically

An Ethics of Sanity

perhaps, because it helps fuel our drive to stand against whatever oppression we genuinely feel victimised by. This clinging to victimhood is a necessary stage in the emancipation of our spirits from the colonisation of society, and as a starting point for radicalisation it is often essential. This is a real value of identity politics - one among the many. And as something informing solidarity with others also wounded by society's cruelties, whether by the same or by different cruelties, identity politics has the potential not only to empower specific communities, but to fill in the gaps in the old grand narratives concerning different oppressions, gaps through which many communities have often slipped into the abyss.

But how do we keep ourselves from becoming stuck at the initial, narrow nationalist stage? How do we ensure our growth from realising our own particular oppression to a sympathy with others affected by oppressions dissimilar to ours? How do we avoid falling into the trap of thinking our own victimisation is "harder to deal with" than another's?

A simple parable might shed light on these questions. Consider any abusive family as an allegory for this civilisation. The father comes home drunk every night to his house, beats his wife black and blue, then staggers into his teenage daughter's room, rapes her repeatedly before staggering back to his own bed. Other nights, he beats up his ten year old son before falling into his drunken torpor. There is a young baby, perhaps one or two years old, who is neglected in her crib most of the time, not fed often, left to cry and lay in her own wastes. The family dog is also neglected and abused, taking the brunt of the frustrations of all in the family.

The question arises: Who in the family is the most oppressed? Or, put another way, who in the family would you least like to be?

These questions may seem very important. Understanding the pain and trauma of each of the "positions" within the society of this nuclear family may well be essential to the eventual healing of the battered wife, the molested daughter, the beaten son, the neglected baby, and the abused dog. But in another sense, these questions are beside the point. The enemy is the same, even if he victimises the members of the household in different ways. And while the ways of maturing mandate different psychological tasks for each in the family, the ultimate direction is clear. Before the wife succumbs to despair; before the daughter commits suicide in order to escape her trauma; before the son grows up to learn to repeat the patterns of abuse of his father; before the baby starves or succumbs to sickness; before the dog dies, drowned by the father in the bathtub during one of his blackouts - before all this happens, *the father must be dealt with.* And, as he sleeps the dead sleep of drunken torpor, any object - even one as innocuous as the pillow each of the family has cried into over the years of horror and oppression - can be used as a weapon of liberation. No "revolutionary class" need be mobilised as the sole agent of revolutionary action. *Anyone* in the family - regardless of the specifics of the oppressions suffered - can mobilise himself or herself to the only task at hand: all can arise from the ruins of trauma, the bloody beds where evil and tyranny has forced them to lie prostrate and helpless - take the pillow from those beds, and smother the drunken monster in his stupor.

A short moment later, power has been removed; the state, the patriarchy, the brute force of privilege has been eliminated. The family then must begin to learn to live freely and autonomously, their old solidarity serving as the basis for the new family relations, replacing the old order of fear, hatred, and isolation.

We are all from this dysfunctional family.

An Ethics of Sanity

Families - the nuclear, isolated islands lost in planned and gated suburbia - are the original site of training for living in an authoritarian, unequal, unjust society. They are the first locus of the inculcation of all the privileges, the schisms, the engineered social roles that are later reinforced in schools, churches, workplaces, armies, etc. These prejudices are the core of our civilised delusion.

The lack of nurturing love most all of us suffer, beginning with parents and siblings who view us not as unique, free snowflakes, but as extensions of their own power (even our names are chosen for us, assigned to us, along with all the social baggage of gender, creed, age, "normative" sexuality, etc., foisted on us before we even know who we are). In order to deal with the traumas of growing into our social roles - or, more authentically, to reject them and begin to define ourselves *for ourselves* - a phase of self-reflection and self-exploration is quintessentially necessary. For many of us, this involves at some point recognising and affirming our particular identities, with all the revolutionary potentials they have for us and for our world. Identity politics are a necessary stage in the development of a revolutionary autonomy for most people. Exploring oneself is not simply "therapeutic" or an apolitical pursuit of "lifestyle"; for most all of us, and particularly those of us who daily contend with dehumanisation based on our given social roles, the exploration of identity is a prerequisite for any further revolutionary work. To discount politics of identity is to deny the very real forces which invalidate most people, and to deny further their means of addressing the problem and coming to wholeness.

It is not my business to tell someone struggling with a social role I am not affected by how to deal with the dystonic voices accompanying those roles. But I can offer one suggestion in the working out of these politics. I have been victimised by my status as a queer, having dealt with many subtle indignities and even occasional violence because of it. But I have also reaped the benefits of maturity and self-love and just plain fun that has come with embracing queerness, despite the victimisation. I have been victimised also by my status as a "madman." Madness has oppressed me both socially and legally, as well as within the dark regions of my innermost self. Yet I have also reaped benefits of insight from it, and learned to love myself better by knowing myself better. My madness has become a part of my radicalism, my spirituality, my love-relationships. It has given me a large measure of my optimism, my hope.

There is a temptation (and I have often fallen into it) to proclaim my experience as superior to that of others outside of the above delineations. And for a time, such an attitude was necessary to counter the negativity accompanying these statuses. Just as Malcolm X initially had to throw out the white identity as evil in order to affirm blackness as beautiful, before he could consider whiteness not the province of melanin essentialism but rather a political mindset which he saw transcended by blond-haired, blue-eyed Muslim men who befriended him in Mecca; just so, I had to hate the straight, hate the sane, in order to love my queerness and my madness, which the former mindsets so marginalise and despise.

All identity politics run the risk of "narrow nationalism," of getting stuck and self-satisfied at the stage of initial reaction against the negative dialectic of socially enforced roles. But people are never static entities; rather, they are processes, ever-changing, ever-building upon previous experiences to form a more whole subjectivity. We must work out our processes the best we can, and all of us could learn better how to be patient with one another during the working out of this process. To deny people their right to concentrate on the oppressions which effect them directly, to work out their political relationship to others and to the civilisation as a whole as they choose to and at the pace they decide, is not only insensitive and unrealistic. It is to stand with the oppressor against them, to in fact in your small way *become the oppressor* in their lives.

Nobody has "the answer." This is the fallacy of claiming one's own analysis as privileged over other people's analyses. (In claiming privilege, after all, be it for your politics or your religion or your specific status, you are doing exactly that - *claiming privilege* - and thus you are exerting power over everyone else.) Your paradigm is correct - for *you*. Of course it is! You would never have adopted it as your own if it weren't. What some recent lines of thought, including the embryonic Mad Pride perspective, have offered us is the valuing of pluralism and the realisation of relativism - even to the point of admitting to a plurality of perception of reality itself. In terms less dramatic than madness - even when a broad, "consensus reality" can be conceded - it is simply a fact of life that every person in the world is living in a slightly (or greatly) different narrative of that world from anybody else.

I early on employed the term "snowflake" to describe this truth, and the metaphor bears a further explanation. From a distance, a snowstorm is one entity, at times a very powerful one. It can stop traffic, down power-lines, turn the course of key battles of entire wars; in short, one snowstorm can change the course of history. The same is true for revolutions. Historians tend to note the actions of great groups of people as decisive "events" in the course of our civilisation's development. Yet, each of these revolutions - pick any one you like - was not the "American Revolution" or the "French Revolution" or the "Red Revolution." It was a vast meeting of minds, hearts, and bodies to accomplish a common goal - a goal that has always been the same: the overthrowing of tyranny.

Every flake of snow that falls is a unique event. It has never happened before, and it will never happen again - in all the history of this planet. Yet snowstorms are events in which the uniqueness of each snowflake may well be lost in overview. As revolutionaries, we can never lose sight of either perspective - the power of the storm, and the integrity and uniqueness of each and every individual who make the storm. How society's madness plays out in the madness of each person's individual narrative can never be duplicated or predicted—and it never should be! Part of the phenomenal beauty of the human species, of all species, of all natural events - living and non-living - is the incredible, precious uniqueness of each entity. There are no "standards" in Nature, no normative types, no thing quite like any other. This is part of the adventure of being alive - the chance every day to experience everything for the first and only time, to learn, to grow, to love. Nobody will fault you for missing these opportunities, of course. But if you miss the opportunity, it is gone forever. And if you live aware of it all, you will touch the ecstasy of existence every single day. Life becomes a Heaven - even if the atheists are right, and no afterlife exists, you can be in it right here on earth - each moment an eternity, for the rest of your natural life.

Standardisation of objects is central to capitalism, indeed to any society based on mass production and consumption. Standardisation of people, their jobs, their faiths, their visions - these go hand in hand with capitalism, and all civilised existence. It is not a mistake that the institutions of social control – work places, schools, many churches, armies, prisons, insane asylums, etc. - attempt to rob people of the

An Ethics of Sanity

opportunities to experience each day as unique and new. These institutions impose routines, standardised patterns of behaviour, space, and time - and it is no accident that human life lived within these institutions is one of misery. The standards are further impressed onto our consciousness of ourselves, our identities reduced to some exterior thing which is then ranked against other standards. The tendency exists even in radical attempts to break this cycle. Thus, we speak of an "anarchist lifestyle" - a particular look, a particular pattern of living, even a particular set of beliefs - which we then apply to others in judgement of their authenticity as anarchists; we may even fit ourselves into this mould, even when we are not entirely conscious of it.

As a closing thought, let us consider the uniqueness of everything in life, of every human being, and allow for that snowflake to be exactly as it is. In the light of this, it seems to me absurd to demand one standard of anyone - even if that standard is my own. I would love it, of course, if the world's people rejected civilised delusions and came to live anarchically, equally, lovingly. But I would *not* want them to do it as *I* do, to feel as I do - at least not in my best, least selfish moments. Anarchy for me is the state where there are no standards, where each subjectivity can grow with all others in a practical harmony. It is finally not a question of changing ourselves into anarchists, as it is accepting and loving ourselves for the natural anarchy already in us, and working together to abolish all social constraints on realising this basic, human reality. My style of anarchy, of radicalism, is not yours - it cannot be, and it *should not be.* A world full of myself would be my vision of Hell, derived from one of my most frightening visions during the crisis of my madness: a room full of mirrors, from which I can never escape, and wherever I turn, I am my only companion. Other people are not Hell, as

Sartre said in *No Exit*; rather, interaction with others, learning from them, giving and receiving love - all of it is what keeps us sane. Hell is isolation, distance, paranoia, the negative side of madness. The gift of a world outside ourselves, the natural world, other creatures, comrades and friends, the people - this can ground us and keep us from spiralling off into the dead-end labyrinth of mental abstraction. Liberation from the tyranny of abstraction is part of the work we must do to find our revolutionary sanity. Working out our individuation, our process of coming to wholeness - both within ourselves and with one another - this is the definition of sanity, a sanity which embraces each of our unique madnesses as the means to our individual health. And, in this process of discovering our individual sanity, we find reasons to work towards a collective sanity for our species and all the planet, affirming the hope of our emancipation from an empire of despair.